RICHARD WINTERS, M.D.

YOU'RE
THE
LEADER

NOW WHAT?

Leadership Lessons from Mayo Clinic

MAYO CLINIC PRESS

MAYO CLINIC PRESS
200 First St. SW
Rochester, MN 55905
MCPress.MayoClinic.org

The information in this book is true and complete to the best of our knowledge. Information in this book is offered with no guarantees. The author and publisher disclaim all liability in connection with the use of this book. The views expressed are the author's personal views, and do not necessarily reflect the policies or position of Mayo Clinic.

To stay informed about Mayo Clinic Press, please subscribe to our free e-newsletter at mcpress.mayoclinic.org or follow us on social media.

For bulk sales to employers, member groups, and health-related companies, contact Mayo Clinic at SpecialSalesMayoBooks@mayo.edu.

Proceeds from the sale of Mayo Clinic Press books benefit medical education and research at Mayo Clinic.

Original illustrations by Richard Winters.
Cover and text design by Barbara Aronica-Buck/Booktrix.

Credits and permissions are listed on page 319.

ISBN 978-1-893005-70-9
Library of Congress Control Number: 2022934405
Printed in the United States of America

CONTENTS

Preface   5

Introduction   7

Part One: Effective Leadership Tactics   17

    Chapter One: Recognize the Limits of Your Expertise   18

    Chapter Two: Map Your Decisions   33

    Chapter Three: Step Up to the Balcony   61

    Chapter Four: Understand Burnout and Well-Being   76

    Chapter Five: Amplify Engagement   95

    Chapter Six: Lead During One-to-One Conversations   127

Part Two: Lead in Complex Situations   159

    Chapter Seven: ROW Forward   160

    Chapter Eight: Document Your Perspectives   175

    Chapter Nine: Create a Shared Reality   194

    Chapter Ten: Identify Fears and Worries   218

    Chapter Eleven: Create a Shared Vision   232

    Chapter Twelve: Generate Multiple Options   243

    Chapter Thirteen: Champion the Way Forward   257

    Chapter Fourteen: Now What?   289

Resources   283

Acknowledgments   284

About the Author   286

About Mayo Clinic   287

Notes   289

Index   309

For you, a leader.

PREFACE

Leadership is difficult. If you're like me and the leaders I coach, you're looking for clues on how to be more effective. I've written this book to provide ideas, tactics, and frameworks to help you deal with your most difficult challenges.

At Mayo Clinic, my colleagues and I care for patients with difficult medical problems. To accomplish our mission, we learn to lead as we face complex challenges. Our most effective leaders know when to quickly and expertly decide, and alternatively, when it's better to take a moment to consider and facilitate.

I suspect you also work in a volatile, uncertain, complex, and often ambiguous environment in which competition, regulations, workforce needs, technologies, and customer demands are in constant flux. In such an environment it is often not enough to simply rely on your own expertise to make decisions. Instead you need to facilitate a more effective approach. This can be learned, and it can be coached.

I am an emergency physician at Mayo Clinic in Rochester, Minnesota. I am also an executive coach for leaders at Mayo Clinic, and director of leadership development for the Mayo Clinic Care Network. I am a tiny star amid a constellation in a high-functioning organization.

I create development programs for Mayo Clinic leaders and the leaders of value-aligned organizations that have partnered with Mayo Clinic. We ask participants to bring their thorniest, most difficult, and emotionally charged problems, and then we provide the framework to help them find their own solutions. It is in this spirit that I write this book for you, a leader, or one in the making.

Please question and challenge what you read. Please investigate and learn from the wise individuals I mention in the text. Please read this book to find the answers and the approaches that elevate your own organization. And have a bit of fun.

Richard Winters
Rochester, Minnesota

INTRODUCTION

Your colleagues are seated around the table, and all eyes are on you as you enter the conference room.

You face a complex challenge, and everyone has a different view of the key factors as well as how to proceed. Nevertheless, it's up to you to move things forward. How you make this decision will affect the way you and your colleagues work together, the success of your organization, and potentially whether you succeed or fail as a leader.

You take your seat and begin, projecting confidence and authority as you address the assembled team.

"Thank you for coming, everyone. We have a big challenge before us and limited time to discuss our options. I'd like to hear from everyone here. What do you think we should do?"

With that, the discussion begins to circle the table, with each person giving their best advice. Several of your colleagues make stirring, eloquent statements about the problem as they see it and their solution of choice. You make sure to keep your eyes on each speaker, nodding and acknowledging each contribution.

Then, finally, the meeting circles back to you. You pause for a moment, and say, "Thank you all for sharing your thoughts. I appreciate your experience, your different perspectives, and your insights. However, after careful consideration, I've come to the conclusion that you're all incorrect. We will proceed with my plan."[1]

You Are Not Alone

If this process for decision-making sounds familiar, rest assured, you're not alone. Perhaps you have made decisions like this. Perhaps you were a participant in a meeting where you volunteered your opinion, and your ideas were summarily shot down.

Leadership plays out this way every day, in every industry, in teams and organizations of every size. No matter what the problem at hand may be, the solution is usually driven by *fiat*—the decision and orders of the leader—or at most by a consensus of only a few.

A top-down process for decision-making by edict may work fine in predictable situations or during times of crisis. But when it comes to making strategic decisions in complex and unpredictable environments, the all-too-familiar method of reflexive decision-making breaks down and delivers poor results. Our expertise and our power to decide get in the way of optimal outcomes. This occurs not only when we lead groups of people, but also when we have one-to-one conversations with colleagues.

Complex Challenges

Think of the complex challenges you face:

- Perhaps you are the product manager. The technology team and the marketing team disagree on the key features for a new and innovative product. This project is vital to the future success of your organization. How do you bring the two sides together to establish a collaborative workflow that sets the strategy, road map, and feature definitions for the product?
- Perhaps you are the chief executive officer of a technology startup. Your colleagues look to you for advice and guidance

about promotion, burnout, career opportunities, disruptive interactions with colleagues, and a litany of other complex personal and organizational challenges. How do you approach your colleagues during these one-to-one conversations to help them achieve their best?

- Perhaps you are the chief medical officer of a hospital. An influential physician approaches you in the hallway to confide that the cardiology group is considering leaving the hospital to work with the competition unless a new cardiac catheterization suite is built. Meanwhile, the existing suites are underutilized, and procedures aren't starting on time. How do you work with the cardiology group to strengthen the partnership and consider mutually beneficial options?

- Perhaps you are the incoming chair of an academic department. While traditional aspects of the department are thriving, new technology and changing environments threaten future success. How do you respect the current power structures and processes, yet move forward with bold and forward thinking?

- Perhaps you are a talented and busy executive sitting in yet another meeting, discussing important issues, though nothing ever seems to change. You feel burned out. How do you push for transformation?

Each strategic challenge involves different perspectives, volatile environments with high stakes, dynamic and ambiguous information, and unpredictable outcomes. These situations are complex. During these times your checklists are inadequate, and your organization will not fly with the smooth precision and predictable steps of an aircraft. These are times when your expertise and best practices are insufficient, and the problem to be solved is a challenge to even define.

What This Book Offers

Whether you are the boss and you call all the shots, a servant leader who empowers others to decide, or an individual without a "title" seeking to make a difference as you sit in yet another meeting, this book will provide you specific tactics to improve your effectiveness in one-to-one conversations and as you lead large teams and organizations.

You will learn the specific techniques I use when coaching leaders and facilitating teams at Mayo Clinic.[2] You will draw on the collective wisdom of colleagues, develop leaders, and achieve results. You will learn to lead in a way that decreases burnout, promotes individual well-being, and sparks engagement.

My hope is that this book both entertains you and helps you achieve results. I will introduce you to leadership thinkers, and I will share mistakes I've made and lessons learned while coaching effective leaders and facilitating effective teams.

Read this book through from start to finish, or pick it up to find a tactic or a process you can use as you face the specific challenges of the moment. The chapters of this book will give you frameworks to guide you and your colleagues through complex challenges. They will prompt you to action.

The first half of the book provides tactics for effective leadership, while the second half lays out the framework for addressing complex situations, as follows:

Part One: Effective Leadership Tactics

1. **Recognize the Limits of Your Expertise.** You are a decision-making machine. As you move throughout your day, you make quick decisions. This is both a feature and a

bug. We think of leaders as deciders who know what to do. But our best leaders recognize when they need to step outside their immediate perspectives to question their initial instincts. These leaders use a deliberate decision-making process to overcome the limitations of expert analysis.

2. **Map Your Decisions.** Your success as a leader depends on developing individual and organizational strategies that recognize and adapt to complexity. Decisions fall into one of five domains: clear, complicated, complex, chaotic, and confused. You will learn to quickly identify and tailor your decision-making process to the decision domain you're operating in.

3. **Step Up to the Balcony.** Each of us has blind spots in our perspective of the world. We are trapped within the biases of our own stories, our need to be right, our seeking of agreement, our sense of control, and our ego. You will learn how to "step off the dance floor" away from your reflexive reactions and "step up to the balcony" to broaden your perspective and make better, more informed decisions.

4. **Understand Burnout and Well-Being.** You will develop an understanding of the specific drivers of burnout and recognize burnout's negative effects on both the personal and professional lives of colleagues. You will learn specific individual, interpersonal, and organizational actions you can take to recognize and improve the Six Dimensions of Psychological Well-Being.

5. **Amplify Engagement.** There are eight specific leadership behaviors proven to decrease burnout and increase

satisfaction in the workplace. You will learn specific behaviors—the DRIVERS of engagement—to more effectively develop, recognize, inform, value, engage, respect, and supervise colleagues. You will learn how to model the specific values-based behaviors that build organizational culture.

6. **Lead During One-to-One Conversations.** Your colleagues are independent thinkers. During one-to-one conversations, effective leaders put aside their expertise. They focus on promoting the organization's strategy and on listening, understanding, and helping colleagues develop their own perspectives and solutions. You will learn the "five hats"— the different approaches of teacher, mentor, coach, supervisor, and sponsor. You will gain the conversational tactics that help colleagues develop the skills, behaviors, and reasoning needed for success. You will learn how to dynamically change your conversational approach to meet the needs of colleagues in the moment.

Part Two: Lead in Complex Situations

1. **ROW Forward.** This framework addresses complex challenges. You work with colleagues to develop a shared **reality** and vision, and then to generate multiple **options** for how to proceed; and then you lead the **way forward**. You may apply the ROW Forward framework in a matter of minutes or hours, or to facilitate multi-day retreats.

2. **Document Your Perspectives.** Effective leaders carve out time and space for uninterrupted thinking about complex challenges. They clarify their thinking and avoid proceeding

ROW Forward Framework

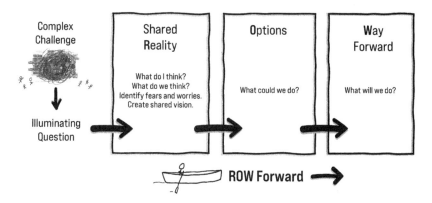

impulsively. You will learn a specific six-step process of recognizing and considering complex challenges.

3. **Create a Shared Reality.** Effective leaders bring colleagues together to help them look around blind spots. They tap into the experience of those inside and outside of the room as they seek to build collective wisdom. You will learn to use a predictable process to bring the diverse and at times contentious perspectives of colleagues together in a manner that adapts to the context, intensity, and time frame of your challenging decisions.

4. **Identify Fears and Worries.** You and each of your colleagues have fears and worries about what might occur as you face a complex challenge. Effective leaders shine light on these worries and bring them to the forefront of decision-making. They know that unacknowledged fears undermine efforts.

5. **Create a Shared Vision.** The mission and values of organizations are frequently stated but often disregarded or

forgotten. Effective leaders authentically infuse the mission and values of their organization into their decision-making. You will learn a process to clarify intention and mitigate perceived risks as you authentically energize and align your colleagues toward a common purpose.

6. **Generate Multiple Options.** After creating shared reality and vision, effective leaders and their colleagues brainstorm multiple options for how they might respond to their complex challenges. You will learn how to choose the best options for ways to move forward. You will also recognize how to predict and defuse the challenging situations that arise when individuals disagree, attempt to block forward movement, or when the decision is not unanimous.

7. **Champion the Way Forward.** The most dangerous moment in the decision-making process happens when everyone walks out of the room and heads back to their routine. Will the decision survive? You will learn several specific practices to ensure that tasks are completed, key learning is re-incorporated back into the decision-making process, and insights are channeled to create further success for yourself and your team in the evolving complex environment.

8. **Now What?** You will convert ideas to action as you identify specific steps you will take to become a more effective leader.

A Caveat

We need leaders who are independent thinkers. There are times when a leader needs to make decisions despite the perspectives of colleagues. In these situations, a group's common sense may lack vision. A fear of the unknown may prevent a team from finding the fortitude needed to adapt to the changing environment. An effective leader provides the strength and the determination to nudge colleagues through the discomfort of change.

Whether you are a leader who prefers to make the final decision, or you favor collective decision-making, my goal is to help you figure out how to effectively leverage the different perspectives of your colleagues—to look behind your own blind spots—as you decide.

Why Lead?

This book is meant to be more than a collection of steps or boxes to check off in the leadership process. Instead, as you move through the pages, think not just about *how* to lead, but also *why* you lead.

Lead to align with a purpose. Lead to engage in a mission. Lead to bring your values to fruition. Seek to increase engagement and the success of those around you. You have an opportunity to improve the lives of your colleagues, your organization, and the people you serve.

Change and challenge are constant. Whether you face a corporate team, a group of investors, or your customers, a structured approach will help you to help them. Together you'll find the way forward and you will be the leader your team needs in the moment.

This book will guide you through those times when colleagues disagree, emotions run high, the environment is turbulent, and it's time to do something. It's for those times when you look at yourself in the mirror and you think, "You're the leader. Now what?"

PART ONE

EFFECTIVE LEADERSHIP TACTICS

1

RECOGNIZE THE LIMITS
OF YOUR EXPERTISE

Dalia has excelled as vice president of operations for a large multinational hospitality company. She's helped the hotelier grow from eight locations nationally to fifty-three locations worldwide. Recently, she's jumped at the opportunity to become the CEO of a boutique hotel company. She looks forward to leveraging her expertise to expand this hotelier, which has an irreverent, adventurous, and young-at-heart character.

Dalia is a no-nonsense, highly educated, and well-informed leader. Making decisions is usually easy for her. She knows what to do and she's rarely stumped. These qualities have served her well throughout her career. Among her friends she is known for her encyclopedic level of knowledge and her ability to bring forward obscure, but essential facts about critical areas of business. She reflexively knows what to do next. She is quick to decide, and has a bias for action.

However, difficulties await Dalia if she approaches her new role solely as a knowledgeable expert. There will certainly be times when she needs to decide quickly, based on her expertise and experience. But at other times Dalia needs a different approach. She should pause, quiet her judgment, and expand her perspective. Those are the moments when she needs to tap into the collective wisdom of her colleagues to collaboratively make sense of challenges. The question is when, and under what circumstances, should she apply each approach? These first two chapters of this book will explore this conundrum: when should a leader simply decide, and when would a more inclusive method of decision-making be more effective?

Decision-Making Machines

We are decision-making machines. Like programmed robots, we respond instantly to input as we go about our daily lives.

Consider a typical morning as an example.

You start making decisions the moment you wake up each day. You decide whether to get up or snooze a little longer. You decide what to eat for breakfast and what beverage to drink. If you work away from home, you decide whether you need an umbrella or a coat as you leave for the office. When you arrive at your workspace, you choose which tasks to prioritize, which meetings you'll attend, who needs to be involved. You make these decisions reflexively.

Now, imagine that you walk into the wrong meeting room, still a bit dull and not entirely awake, and you encounter the following unexpected situation. On your left you see a baby; on your right you see an angry wolf. You need to quickly decide: which one is safest to pick up and move to safety?

Easy, right? You make a quick decision. You reach for the baby and dash out of the room. Your reflexive response keeps you and the baby safe. The same quick decision-making also keeps you from becoming overwhelmed by the multiple choices we encounter every day.

But what happens when circumstances are not as clear-cut? How do you resolve thorny situations entangled in the uncompromising perspectives of cantankerous colleagues during turbulent times? Do you alter the process of how you decide? Or do you simply make decisions reflexively, just as you did with the wolf and the baby?

As decision-making robots, we have a sentient flaw: we tend to overplay our expertise, and let our expertise guide our actions. But there are times when our robotic reflex to decide short-circuits optimal decision-making.

Think about the last meeting you attended. As you listened to each of your colleagues give their opinions about a novel situation, did you reflexively think, "Yes, I agree." or "No. You are incorrect."? And during this meeting, did one of your colleagues reflexively respond to you?

We form instantaneous opinions based upon our emotions, experiences, and beliefs. And in a split second we may misjudge what a colleague has said. Despite the complexity of the situation, as decision-making robots we are rarely stumped.[1] But that doesn't mean we are always correct or in any way knowledgeable about the circumstances.

The Expert Taskmaster

Victor, the chair of thoracic surgery, is at the top of his field. He's an innovator in the surgical treatment of complex esophageal pathology. He's a mentor to his colleagues. And he frightens the nurses with whom he works.

Each morning as he makes the rounds of his hospitalized patients, the hallways empty. The nurses scatter to safety. They hide in utility closets and they retreat to other hallways. They do anything to avoid interacting with Victor.

Victor firmly believes in a team-based approach to care. He knows that when nurses, social workers, pharmacists, and physicians work closely together, they share critical information, and this improves patient outcomes. Yet among the nurses, Victor is a team of one.

Victor envisions the perfect environment for his patients. He sees himself as the captain of the ship. He believes he bears the ultimate responsibility for life or death, and the voice in his head is a relentless taskmaster—brutally honest, opinionated, and unedited in speaking about what is right and wrong. It knows in a moment with surgical precision what should and what shouldn't be done. When that internal voice becomes his outside voice, it can be ruthless. Its powerful and patronizing tenor has embarrassed and admonished individuals in front of colleagues and even patients. It is a voice that destroys the psychological safety of the care team. A voice that impedes optimal care. A voice that needs further training.

We Overplay Our Expertise

At times our expertise is helpful; at other times it is not.

As an emergency physician, I was trained to walk into a room to care for someone I have never met. I take a brief history, perform a focused exam, and write orders for the care team to complete. After that, I move on to see the next patient. This process repeats itself twenty to thirty times during an average shift.

My ability to leverage expertise and make quick, informed decisions is key to my effectiveness as an emergency physician. I expect that success in your area of expertise also depends on quick decisions.

However, there are times when we overplay our expertise. I know I sometimes do, whether as an emergency physician, a leader, a coach, or a friend. Once I came home to my family after a busy shift. My body was at home, but my mind was still embedded in the rapid pace of the emergency department.

Robot
Me
↓
🧍

	Wife ↓ 🧍	Daughter ↓ 🧍	

I greeted my wife and she brought up a problem she was working through. After listening to a brief history, and without any further discussion or reflection, I knew what she should do, and I told her.

Then I walked into the next room and my daughter brought up an issue she encountered in high school. I was not stumped. I've been to high school. I knew what she should do, and I gave her a list of actions to take care of her issue.

But in both cases I received immediate negative feedback. It quickly became apparent that my expertise and quick decisions were not helpful in this case. My family believed that their issues required an approach different from the process I used in caring for a patient with a kidney stone or a heart attack.

While neither my wife's nor my daughter's problems stumped me, my family's aversion to my input made sense. I did not seek their perspectives. I did not consider the complex dynamics of their own existence. My quick-deciding emergency medicine approach did not translate to the home environment. While I thought I was being helpful, I was not.

In these situations a part of me wants to respond, "Do you know who I am? I'm kind of a big deal around here." But then I imagine my daughter quickly retorting, "Yes. And, no you're not." And she's right, I'm no bigger deal than she is. If my goal is to help my family, I must keep the distorted thoughts of grandeur to myself.

Similarly, I see the decision reflex get overplayed by some of the leaders I coach. These leaders make difficult decisions. Sometimes they face simple "pick up the baby or wolf" scenarios (see page 20), but oftentimes they deal with situations and relationships that are complex, messy, and difficult to understand. Their reflexive decisions as leaders don't incorporate the informed perspectives and experiences of their colleagues. The research chair, the education chair, and the chair of clinical practice have different experiences and perspectives. If one of those chairs responds like a reflexive robot in a shared meeting, they risk disrespecting the perspectives of others. They create an atmosphere that limits opportunities for team success. And if they are fortunate, they get direct feedback about their problematic behavior from their colleagues.

Dalia, the CEO of the boutique hotel, is a knowledgeable expert. Yet her perspectives may differ from her VP of marketing or her VP of operations. Her conversations with these colleagues need to consider their different perspectives. They may help her look around blind spots and spot other opportunities. Dalia must pay attention to not overplay her expertise. She needs to work to be less reflexive, less robotic in her decision-making.

Victor, the thoracic surgeon, is well-intentioned. He truly wants the best for his patients. But he needs to examine how his expertise has created blind spots in his thinking, and how his style of blunt, reflexive communication limits the effectiveness of the healthcare team.

A Snapple Decision

Consider a reflexive decision from the competitive world of consumer products.[2, 3] In 1983, the CEO of Quaker Oats Company decided to purchase Gatorade.[4] The CEO liked Gatorade, and he was a respected expert in the food business. He directed his team to make the acquisition, and it was a success—Gatorade's sales rose from a few hundred million dollars annually to more than a billion dollars per year. Eleven years later, when the same CEO decided he liked Snapple, he leaned again on his expertise and made a similarly quick decision. But that time, his expertise failed.

The CEO drew on his extensive experience and assumptions. During this process, he and his team failed to consider several crucial things: Snapple's distributors held contracts in perpetuity, and they would resist key aspects of the Quaker Oats distribution plan; the bottling volumes for a sports drink differed from those of a mealtime drink and would affect sales projections; and Snapple's quirky culture—a big draw for the brand—would clash with Quaker Oats' suit-and-tie approach.[5] Additionally, the executive team decided to drop several Snapple spokespersons who had large groups of followers in favor of polished mass marketing campaigns.

Each decision Quaker Oats made seemed rational and obvious to their leadership, but failed to incorporate the perspectives of key customers, distributors, and promoters. This hobbled the acquisition from the start. In response to being dropped, one of the spokespersons, the influential radio personality Howard Stern, who had previously been highly effective in advertising the brand, rechristened the product "Crapple" and made the struggling brand a prized topic for frequent on-air rants.

Within a few years, Snapple's sales cratered. In 1997 Quaker Oats sold it off at a loss of $1.4 billion.[6] What followed was an easy decision for Quaker's board: find a new CEO.

Those directors can tell you this: Sometimes expertise is helpful, but sometimes it's woefully ill-suited to the decision at hand. Our own analyses and gut instincts can get in the way of effective deciding.

Process versus Analysis

What is most important when making a decision: process or expert analysis?[7]

If you're like many people I've worked with, you're probably thinking, "they both are," but I'm asking you to pick just one. Which one is most important in improving the effectiveness of decisions?

A study published in the *McKinsey Quarterly* examined 1,048 complex decisions made by managers within large organizations about such things as major acquisitions, investment in new products, and choices of key technologies.[8] First, the researchers asked the managers involved in each decision to estimate their application of various practices of analysis and process. Then they asked the same managers to assess the outcomes of their decisions based upon metrics such as revenue, profitability, market share, and productivity.

The authors found that process is six times more important than analysis in improving decision-making effectiveness. Yes, a leader's analysis—detailed financial modeling, sensitivity analysis, and predictions of the market's reaction—was important. But far more important was the process used to make the decision. Did it include perspectives that contradicted the leader's point of view? Did it capture the input of individuals with varied experiences and skills without regard to their formal rank within the organization?

The fact that process trumps analysis makes sense, doesn't it? Our individual analysis is obscured by blind spots in our expertise. We can create intricate spreadsheets, explore subtle nuances, and deeply consider the possibilities, but still lack the essential data that lurks beyond our own perspective. A decision process that helps us see around blind corners will result in better decisions.

Re-evaluating and improving decisions is essential for advancing medical care. In the past, despite extensive expert analysis, medication errors were alarmingly common. The wrong drug, given to the wrong patient, at the wrong dose, at the wrong time.

For example, previously when a patient presented to the critical care unit with pneumonia, treatment decisions came from the expert analysis of a single physician during a busy shift. The physician would scan through the patient's past medical history, list of allergies, and test results, and then compare a list of local bacteria susceptibilities with the published opinions of experts—all to figure out the antibiotic and dose for treatment. You can imagine that such detailed analysis in a dynamic critical care unit could occasionally result in error, despite best intentions.

In modern critical care units, the electronic health record, clinical pharmacists, and bar code scanners help the care team see through blind spots of individual analysis. The electronic health record (EHR) identifies pertinent allergies, potential medication interactions, and appropriate antibiotic choices. Clinical pharmacists perform independent bedside analysis of each patient's treatment plan. They recognize important variables that the physician, nurse, and electronic health record might miss. Nurses use bar code administration systems to scan each medication and the patient's wristband to ensure that the correct drug is infused. Such improvements help care teams leverage the expert analysis of several professionals to identify the right medication, for the right patient, at the right dose, at the right time.

The Pitfalls of Analysis

In the emergency department I treat patients based upon my expert judgment. I can explain to you the sensitivities and specificities of the tests I order, I can detail the physiology and pathology involved in my differential diagnoses, and I can explain the rationale for each part of my treatment plan. But despite my expert analysis, I can still miss important details.

Did I get input from the family or the paramedics? The pharmacist noticed something in the past medical records that might be important, and the nurse thinks something else might be going on. Did I invite their opinions and listen to them?

When I block out the perspectives and analyses of others as part of my process of caring for patients, no matter how on-point my own siloed analysis is, I am less effective.

The executive team at Quaker Oats performed detailed analysis, no doubt, before each of their actions. But did they seek out the insights of key customers, distributors, and promoters before making their decision? And if they got those perspectives, did they incorporate them into the decision process? Or did they reflexively think, "No. We disagree. We've come to the conclusion that they are all incorrect, and we will proceed with our plan"?

We've all worked with individuals who are deeply analytical—armed with spreadsheets and diagrams and facts—but just don't seem to get the big picture.

When I talk to leaders, I frequently hear about the pitfalls that occur when they rely on their own expert analyses—and it's often a shock to them when it happens. Soon after rising to an executive level at his company, one leader I coached got a question from the CEO about changing the employee health plan. The company needed to cut expenses without jeopardizing care for employees. The leader was new in his role but had been in the industry for more than a decade and felt secure in his expertise. He compared the two health plans using a spreadsheet and saw that there was a 98 percent crossover in approved primary care providers. The new list captured all of the preferred specialists and nearly all of the primary care physicians. This high number resonated with him, and he gave a confident decision to make the switch to the new, cheaper plan.

Turns out he should have been more concerned with that outlying 2 percent.

When the health plan was switched it became clear that the outlying 2 percent represented an influential group of primary care physicians who were now excluded from the options employees could choose. The leader now had a stream of angry employees complaining that the switch had forced them to move from long-term, trusted local providers and specialist physicians. Who cared about the 98 percent overlap? They missed the 2 percent no longer part of their insurance coverage. The leader spent the next two years unraveling his mistake and rebuilding trust.

He had overplayed his expertise. His confidence in his own background led him to see the decision as an easier and more direct choice than it really was. He was partially blinded by all that he knew. And he couldn't have been more shocked by this outcome. The damage he did and the time it took to fix came to him as a surprise. After all, he was an expert—who expected such a nightmare?

Put the Brakes on Expertise

You have experience, and knowledge, and opinions, no doubt. But when do you need to put the brakes on your reflexive analysis and adopt a slower, more deliberative process?

Remember Dalia? Will she decide to outsource housekeeping for the boutique hotels? Will she change vendors for the food provided to guests? Where will they locate employee parking? Which ad agency will they choose?

Dalia has instincts for what to do about each question; in a sense, she *knows* what to do. But are her instincts correct? These are not simple questions. Each query contemplates a complex challenge that cannot easily be resolved. Smart people will disagree about what to consider, how to decide, and what the best outcomes might be. During these times Dalia needs to open up the decision process to others. She needs to reframe the way she makes sense of opportunities as she ponders alternative perspectives and scenarios. If, on the other hand, she makes these decisions in the same reflexive way that would lead her to "pick up the baby and not the angry wolf," she will be less effective.

Remember Victor, the intimidating thoracic surgeon? His name is Victor Trastek and he is now an esteemed emeritus professor at Mayo Clinic. With the help of specific feedback from a nurse manager, he gained perspective and changed both his thinking and his approach. He became a champion of professionalism and inter-disciplinary teamwork. A video interview between Dr. Trastek and nurse manager Shelly Olson is shared with new physicians and scientists during their orientation to Mayo Clinic.[9]

Dr. Trastek went on to become the CEO of Mayo Clinic in Arizona and a member of the Mayo Clinic Board of Governors. After an illustrious career, he retired from patient care. He currently serves as an executive coach for Mayo Clinic department chairs.

NOW WHAT?

Think of a decision you are making right now where you might want to put the brakes on your reflexive decision-making and adopt a slower, more deliberate process.

Write down how you might approach the decision in a different manner.

What's Next?

The next chapter will help you map the specific kinds of decisions you make. There are times when your reflexive instinct to decide serves you well, and times when you need to call in other experts. And sometimes you need to slow down the decision process altogether and seek the perspectives of others so that you and your team better address the complexity of the situation.

Executive Summary

➤ We are decision-making machines. We make decisions reflexively even when situations call for a more considered approach.

➤ We form instantaneous opinions based upon our emotions, experiences, expertise, and beliefs. And we are rarely stumped.

➤ We overplay our expertise. Our confidence in our own experience leads us to overestimate our ability to make reasoned decisions in complex environments.

➤ Working on a professional goal can help us identify areas in which our quick decisions may get in the way of our effectiveness.

➤ For complex decisions, process is six times more important than analysis when examining decision-making effectiveness.

➤ Our expert analysis is clouded by our inevitable blind spots. Effective decision processes in complex environments include perspectives that contradict the leader's point of view and seek the input of individuals with varied experiences and skills despite their formal rank within the organization.

2

MAP YOUR DECISIONS

Tension in the clinic is running high. Some physicians are threatening to leave the practice to work at the competition; others are calling for a vote of no confidence in Justin, the clinic's managing partner; and yet others cannot figure out why their colleagues are so riled up.

The Blue Earth Healthy Living Clinic employs 32 physicians to provide care for 80,000 patients each year. They are the premier primary care practice in their region, and while each physician at the clinic is proud of the service they provide, their success and the exponential growth of the city's population have strained the group's ability to deliver their high standard of patient care.

Lately, new patients have encountered a two-month wait when calling to schedule an appointment. As a result, Justin and the other three members of the executive team have decided that the clinic needs to open one hour earlier each morning to accommodate the influx of new patients. This decision has angered many of their colleagues.

Justin, rattled by the dissent, has called an emergency meeting of the executive group to discuss how to proceed.

Prior to the meeting, one member of the executive team surveyed colleagues to understand the discord. She learned that some physicians are scrambling to figure out how to get their kids to school in the morning given the early start time, while others feel they are already working too many hours and risking burnout. Every physician found the action poorly planned and asked, "How could Justin have decided without our input?"

Another member of the executive team suggested an outside consultant to help examine the situation and prescribe needed steps. She noted that many physician groups had experienced similar issues and there was no need to re-invent proven processes. She knew of a similar group, for example, that had leveraged remote technologies, scribes, and innovative staffing models to overcome similar challenges without expanding physician work.

A third member of the team was getting all the more frustrated. "This is ridiculous! We shouldn't re-evaluate our decision. We've been through this before and we can't change our minds every time someone feels uncomfortable. We already discussed this and we added flexibility to the schedule so that people wouldn't need to work more hours. We need to educate the complainers and move on."

Should the executive team push through the immediate discomfort of their colleagues and carry on with their initial decision? Should they hire a consultant? Should they re-consider and invite additional perspectives for ways to move forward?

It's as if Justin and each of the members of the executive team holds a different map of the world as they contemplate how to navigate the same challenge. As a result, their discussion is confused. The executive team needs to share a common map to consider how to migrate through the bumpy terrain of their path forward. Otherwise, opportunities for success will be lost.

Each decision a leader makes resides within a decision-making domain, and each domain requires a different approach. In this chapter, you will learn how to map the different kinds of decisions you and your colleagues make each day. When you recognize the decision domain and apply the correct process, you improve your effectiveness.

The Cynefin Framework

The Cynefin framework created by David Snowden—the founder and chief scientific officer of management consulting firm Cognitive Edge—helps us understand the decision-making environment.[1, 2] Cynefin (say: kuh-nev-in) is the Welsh word for habitat, referring to the framework's purpose of giving decision-makers a conceptual place to stand within the decision habitat—a map—to sort the environment and the demands of the decision process.

According to the Cynefin framework, each decision falls into one of five domains:[3]

- Clear
- Complicated
- Complex
- Chaotic
- Confused

Clear and complicated decisions reside within the realm of the predictable world. Within these domains we can rely upon our experience and expertise as we decide. What we think will occur has a high probability of actually occurring—we can predict the outcome.

On the other hand, complex and chaotic decisions fall within the realm of the unpredictable world. Decisions within this realm yield unpredictable results. Our intended outcomes are possible, but not probable, and definitely not certain. The unpredictable world is the province of volatility, uncertainty, complexity, and ambiguity.

Over the next few pages we will explore each of the Cynefin framework's decision-making domains. You will learn how to recognize where on the map your decisions reside, and in doing so you'll be better prepared to make effective decisions.

Clear Decisions

Clear decisions are easy. When you make clear decisions, the process and likely outcome are obvious to both you and your colleagues. You agree that when *this happens*, we do *this specific thing* and have *this probable outcome*. On the other hand, when *that happens*, we do *that*. The causes and the effects are known and the answer is evident.

Let's return to a question alluded to in the previous chapter as an example of a clear decision: "Do you pick up a baby or an angry wolf?"

If either you or your colleagues walked into a room and saw a baby and an angry wolf, it would be instantly clear to you and your colleagues that you should pick up the baby, and not the angry wolf. The baby is tiny, and giggling, and does not have teeth. The angry wolf is large and snarling with big teeth, and is threatening the baby.

If, on the other hand, one of your colleagues chose to do the non-obvious and picked up the angry wolf, we can clearly predict that the outcome would be suboptimal. Your colleague's choice would likely result in a visit to the emergency department.

Clear decisions may involve single steps (for example, pick up the baby), or they may include sequences of steps. Pilots develop checklist algorithms to make clear decisions before they fly an airplane. The pilot and co-pilot read down the checklist, check off each step, and proceed to the next action. If at the "check engine" step they find that the engine works properly, they move on to the next step. If it does not, there is no argument; the alternative step is clear.

We create *best practices* from clear decisions. If you go to your doctor with a sore throat, they follow multiple common steps as they decide on care. If your physician suspects an uncomplicated sore throat, the next step as part of their best practice algorithm is to consider whether to perform a throat culture. Best practice dictates a culture if you have three or more of the following: an absence of a cough, a temperature greater than 100.4°F (38°C), swollen and painful lymph nodes by your throat, and tonsillar swelling or purulence.[4, 5] Then if the throat culture is positive, your physician will follow best practice to decide which antibiotic to prescribe.

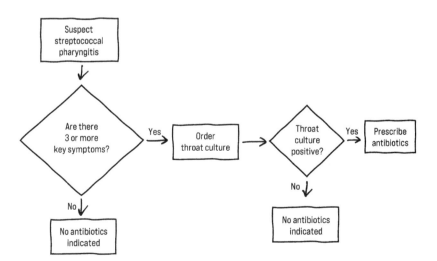

Here are other examples of clear decisions within processes:

- Submitting bugs found in source code.
- Identifying a patient's test results.
- Depositing employee salaries into bank accounts.
- Ordering x-rays for patients with limb fractures.

But some things challenge the clarity of a decision.

Clarity depends on context. The context of our decisions matter. What is *clear* depends upon the participants, the location, the levels of knowledge, the experience, and other relevant factors.

The clear choice for one group of individuals may not be clear to another group of individuals. In the context of the "baby or the wolf" scenario, if your colleagues are *wolf tamers* who *fear babies*, their clear choice may be to pick up the scared wolf, rather than the stinky-diapered, runny-nosed, earlobe-grabbing little human. The best practice for a group of wolf tamers in this situation differs from that of most people based on their expertise and experiences.

The location of a situation also affects clarity. Imagine a patient having a heart attack. In the emergency department, we have detailed best practices to address cardiac arrest. The best practice for the same patient on an airplane or in a remote wilderness, without resources, is quite different.

Best practices are by definition past practices.[6] We develop best practices based upon our experience of what has worked in the past. However, circumstances change. We may find ourselves applying a best practice when the present situation is completely different, and perhaps previously unknown to us.

For example, a best practice of ordering supplies just in time reduces the costs of storing inventory. But this best practice doesn't work if supplies become scarce. At the beginning of the COVID-19 pandemic, hospitals that had relied on just-in-time delivery of protective facemasks ran out of the critical masks much earlier than those hospitals that had stored large backup inventories of masks in preparation for a potential pandemic. Best practices are developed from past experience, and the present setting may be quite different from the past.

We become trapped by entrained thinking.[7] When presented with information, our mind sorts through what to consider and what we have already considered: *This* is relevant, *that* is not. However, if we are not deliberately thoughtful in our approach, we may reflexively rely on past experience and previously developed perspectives as we decide in truly novel situations.

Our entrained thinking, while efficient, has a cost—it blinds us to new ways of making sense of our environment. And as we follow a conditioned path of deciding, we fail to notice that things have changed. We become overconfident in our competence and errantly explain away inconsistencies. What we quickly consider to be irrelevant emerges to become acutely relevant. What has always worked well for us no longer does. We have failed to anticipate and recognize a difficult challenge.[8]

NOW WHAT?

What are examples of clear decisions you face right now?

What are some examples of best practices you used to follow that no longer apply?

Complicated Decisions

Complicated decisions require the analysis and assistance of experts. A complicated domain still has a relationship between cause and effect, but most people can't see it.[9] An expert is needed to help decide the way forward.

When we encounter a complicated issue and have no expertise of our own, we seek the advice of experts and consider their recommendations:

- We ask the marketing team to consider how to best approach the rollout of a new product.
- We ask our regulatory group to recommend the steps we can take to remain compliant with the legal aspects of the actions we consider.
- We ask our children to pick out a gift for their friend's birthday party.

Additionally, and this might surprise you, experts may disagree. Each expert, given the same data, may have a different answer for how to best achieve a desired outcome.

Experts in medicine debate matters all of the time. Ask multiple cardiologists how to treat someone with high blood pressure, and you may get different answers. Alter diet and no medicine; start this medicine, but not that one; use this dosage, not that one; start both of these medicines; monitor and repeat blood pressure readings over the next week, and so on. While the goal of each of the cardiologists is the same (to lower the person's blood pressure and improve their health), the science is intricate with nuanced variables—it is complicated. There may be multiple ways to achieve the same desired outcome.

Complicated decisions have several challenges:

Experts become trapped by entrained thinking. Experts may develop blind spots that lead them to prematurely disregard important variables based on previous analysis and experience. They may develop an overconfident belief in their own thinking. In finding other evaluations of the problem incorrect, and confirming that their plan is the way to go, they may have missed key elements of the changing environment.

Expert: "It is my opinion that we should be wearing several base layers of wool, in addition to mittens, boots, and a hat."

Non-expert: "Really?"

Expert: "Certainly. It is winter and I have extensive experience with winter clothing. This is my recommendation."

Non-expert: "But we are inside and the heat is on."

Paralysis by analysis. Solutions (and needed action) may be delayed due to overthinking and overanalyzing the problem. We may develop an unquenchable thirst for more data, more calculations, more experts, and more of whatever seems relevant in the moment. Meanwhile, the problem remains unsolved.

Paralysis by analysis can be quite common in data-intensive fields.

> Engineer #1: "Show me the data."
>
> Engineer #2: "I don't agree with that data. Here is better data."
>
> Engineer #3: "That data only tells part of the story. We need more data."
>
> Engineer #1: "Where is engineer #4?"
>
> Engineer #2: "They are running a regression analysis on their data."
>
> Engineers #1 and #3: "That will never work."

NOW WHAT?

What are examples of complicated decisions you make for others within your area of expertise?

What are examples of situations in which you consult experts to make complicated decisions?

When have you experienced entrained thinking or analysis paralysis?

Entering the VUCA World

Up to this point, we've considered decisions for which cause and effect are discoverable, and the outcomes are probable. While there may be a single correct answer (use the left blinker to signal a left turn) or multiple correct answers (use this medication or that one to lower blood pressure), we can with confidence predict the results of our actions. We can rely on our expertise and the expertise of others.

But increasingly the decision world is not so tidy. We face situations in which the variables and the outcomes are murky. We encounter situations in which the forces at play are unknowable, the data incomplete, and the outcomes unpredictable despite our expertise. We may have a general idea about what we would like to do, but our colleagues seems to have a completely different perspective about what is occurring and what is possible.

During these uncomfortable situations we are likely to be in the domains of complexity or chaos. These domains lie within the realm of VUCA—where **v**olatility, **u**ncertainty, **c**omplexity, and **a**mbiguity are the norm.[10, 11]

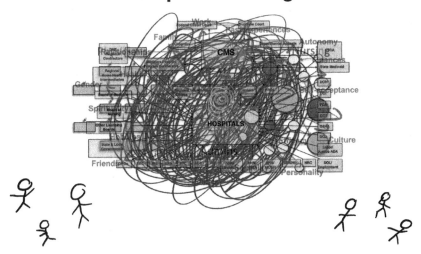

Complex Challenge

Living in the VUCA World

Increasingly we live and work in a VUCA world.[12] In the following scenario let's consider how each of the components of the VUCA acronym might arise during an imagined day at work.

Volatile

Volatile environments change suddenly and unexpectedly.

You go to work with a plan for the day and a list of To-Dos to complete by lunch. Then as you sit down in your workspace, you receive a call from the school: "Your child has a fever and is coughing." As you begin to walk toward your secretary to discuss rescheduling your first meetings so that you can leave the office and pick up your child, your colleague stops you in the hall: "We need you in here now. Our biggest client is considering going with another firm on this project." This turbulence with the client could threaten a big chunk of your business. So you agree to drop by in person for ten minutes and then continue the discussion on the phone while you drive to pick up your child, but first you need to talk to your secretary. And you arrive at your secretary's desk to find an empty seat.

Uncertain

In uncertain situations, information is unpredictable and difficult to interpret when it comes into view.

As you drive to pick up your sick child from school, you wonder, "Why is your biggest client considering another firm for this project? Are they considering moving the rest of their portfolio to the competition? What is it about the competition that is so compelling?" Then as you pull into the driveway of the school you think about your child and hope they recuperate quickly. You wonder whether you are a good parent, because while you definitely want your child to be safe and comfortable, you feel preoccupied with work. This leads you to wonder whom you might call to take care of your child while you try to figure out the issue with your client.

Complex

Complex settings have many interconnected and variable parts.

You find out that your biggest client is considering three firms for the project. The other two firms are larger than your organization and they have significant resources. Additionally, you recently heard that those two competing firms were already partnering in several spaces. You and the board of directors had been considering approaching one of the competing firms to discuss a potential merger. But your board is divided, so you decide to assemble a board meeting to discuss the situation. At the same time, you decide to take your child to be seen by their primary care physician. But that physician is sick, and your child, who feels miserable and is in tears, does not want to see anyone else. And where is your secretary?

Ambiguous

Ambiguous challenges can be interpreted in multiple different ways.

You take your child to a different primary care physician. They tell you that it could be a virus and that no tests are needed at this time. You're told to wait to see how things go. If there is no improvement, then they may need to do more testing, as the illness could be caused by bacteria or something else.

In the meantime, your board is conflicted with how to approach the concerns related to the competition. Some see the situation as reflecting larger national and global movements within the industry. They point out potential regulatory issues and possible barriers related to certain political interests. Others see the current situation as simply reflecting a best practice of business—that your biggest client is merely seeking proposals from competing groups in order to consider the best rates, offerings, and services. These directors think it is simply up to you to reassert the strong relationship that you already have with the client—and they wonder why you called an emergency board meeting.

VUCA Chess

So how do you make decisions when you encounter a VUCA environment? VUCA challenges involve an interplay of technologies, systems, cultures, relationship structures, beliefs, perspectives, and environments, and they take place at the local, regional, national, and international levels. All of this impacts the effectiveness of actions you may take.

The VUCA environment scoffs at individual expertise. It taunts those of us who attempt to methodically predict and plot moves. And yet many of us are guilty of applying methodical chess-like thinking as we manage our organizations. We think we can leverage our knowledge and experience to plot our moves and outplay our challenges. If we see five moves ahead, we will outplay an opponent who sees only two moves ahead. If we see seven moves ahead, even better. We are entrained in thinking, "Okay, so first we will make this move and then they will respond like this. Then we'll do that." We think we can plan each move in advance and analyze the situation ahead of time, and that this will lead to success.

The VUCA environment does not play a dignified match of royal chess; it plays VUCA chess.[13] As we consider our next seven moves, another VUCA chessboard appears and all of a sudden, as we attempt to adjust our strategy, our opponent starts taking our pieces. Then, while we are still thinking, our own pieces start to move independently to other chessboards as they take our own pieces in addition to those of the challenger. There are multiple chessboards with multiple different players, and we are enmeshed in the immediately unknowable and unpredictable. Our step-by-step strategy is no longer applicable. The rules and the state of our environment are volatile, uncertain, complex, and ambiguous.

VUCA Domains

When we face VUCA challenges we are in the unpredictable domains of either chaos or complexity. In both domains, a leader is unable to prescribe or predict the outcomes of decisions. The data is unclear, evolving, and can be interpreted in multiple ways. There are many interconnecting forces interacting in emerging environments—both inside and outside of the organization. Best practices no longer apply, and expertise is misleading. During these VUCA challenges, we need to approach decisions in a different manner. We need to lead in a different way.

Decision-making within the domains of chaos versus complexity differ in both the amount of time available to make the decision and the process used to make the decision.

The Unpredictable VUCA Domains

Chaos
- Little time to consider
- Leader decides in a moment and moves quickly to action

Complexity
- Time to consider and explore
- Leader surveys the many perspectives of colleagues before moving to action

During the crisis of chaos, time is limited. A leader needs to step up and decide the course of action in a matter of seconds to hours. There is little time to consult the perspectives of close colleagues, and there is no time to gain the broader perspectives of those beyond an immediate circle. The leader must take the limited information they have and rely on their experience, expertise, and gut instinct to decide on an immediate action.

In contrast, decisions made in complex situations evolve over the course of days to months. A leader has time to assume a facilitation role and step up to the challenge with groups of colleagues to survey the broader perspectives of many. There is time to develop a shared reality and to explore the nuances of the complex challenge before moving to action.

We will explore the differences of approach to chaos and complexity as we progress further, especially in Part Two of the book.

Decisions in Chaos

Welcome to chaos:

- An emerging virus suddenly sickens 35 percent of your workforce.
- Over the course of two days, an influential newspaper publishes an article that undercuts your corporate strategy, a board member is imprisoned, and a key leader leaves to work for a competitor.
- A product recall abruptly limits an essential material in your supply chain, and the alternative distributor, overwhelmed with inquiries, is not answering your requests.
- An earthquake decimates the town where your warehouse is located.

In chaotic environments, an unforgiving taskmaster towers over you with a stopwatch. You'd like to get more input. You cannot. You'd like to have a better understanding of what is occurring. You cannot. You'd like to prepare your resources to better meet the challenge. You cannot. The taskmaster of chaos demands an immediate response.

In the VUCA domain of chaos, leaders need to create order from disorder. They need to rely on their experience, their expertise, and their senses to make the best decision despite the unknowable situation. They need to stop the bleeding. They need to stand up and say "This is what we need to do."

As effective leaders apply their decisions during the crisis of chaos, they test the environment and its response to their actions. While some aspects of the environment will remain murky and unknowable, other aspects will begin to reveal areas of order and clarity. And as order is identified, experts can articulate what is knowable and predictable, and eventually develop best practices.

In early 2020, as the COVID-19 virus rapidly developed into a worldwide pandemic, leaders around the world were challenged to respond immediately to the chaotic environment. They had no time to consider. They needed to react.

At Mayo Clinic, for example, CEO Gianrico Farrugia and the senior leadership team needed to make quick decisions to bolster the healthcare organization's ability to care for large numbers of patients with acute severe illness, while mitigating the losses from a decrease in non-urgent patient visits.

- The salaries of senior leaders, physicians, and scientists were cut while work pressures increased; many administrative colleagues within the organization were placed on furlough; and retirement benefits were placed on hold.

- All patients, staff, and visitors were screened for symptoms of COVID; mask-wearing was immediately required for all employees and visitors; and personal protective equipment such as high-filtration masks were rationed.
- Non-urgent surgeries and many in-person clinic visits were postponed; telemedicine and testing equipment were purchased; and research and clinical taskforces were set up to coordinate pandemic-related activities.

Decisions were made thoughtfully and quickly. But they were difficult. There was no time to seek the perspectives of 65,000 employees. There was no time to consult all of the leaders in the formal organization chart. The senior leaders stepped up to the challenge, as did leaders of organizations throughout the world.

Effective Leadership during the Crisis of Chaos

There are several actions you can take to lead effectively during a crisis of chaos.

Act with Urgency

Effective leaders step up and make difficult decisions in the highly volatile, uncertain, complex, and ambiguous environment of chaos. They rely on their experience, their expertise, and their senses to make the best decision despite the unknowable situation.

Leverage Your Leadership Team

During a crisis of chaos, effective leaders don't have the time to set up a series of meetings to assemble the perspectives of colleagues deep within the organization; however, they do take advantage of the wisdom and perspectives of close colleagues. When possible, even simple pro-versus-con discussions with immediate colleagues can help the leader clarify thinking and action.

Delegate Decisions

Effective leaders delegate the decision-making for areas of expertise to the experts. For example, the decision on how to best create a safe environment for patient care at Mayo Clinic during the COVID-19 epidemic was delegated to a taskforce of infectious disease specialists. Even though the infectious environment was unknowable in the earliest stages of the pandemic, this group was best positioned to consider the unknowns associated with COVID-19 infectivity.

Admit Vulnerability

By definition, the domain of chaos is unknowable. This means that decisions are made based on incomplete information with limited perspectives. During these situations, effective leaders are humble, open, and realistic.[14] They discuss what they do not know and admit when they've made a mistake.[15]

Liberate Time for Deliberate Focus

Effective leaders give their teams permission to cancel routine meetings so that they may focus on their response to the crisis. They give colleagues the power to triage what is immediately important and what is not. They liberate time so that colleagues may adapt to the crisis with deliberate focus.

Be Transparent and Communicate

Leaders must communicate what is known and what is unknown. Each of the steps taken during a response to crisis needs to be translated to colleagues. Without transparent communication, rumor and misinformation fill the silence. Simple bullet-pointed messages, video briefings, and targeted face-to-face interviews and visits can communicate succinctly during a crisis.

Bring the Backchannel Forward

The backchannel is the place of hidden and informal conversation. It is where colleagues communicate among themselves as they attempt to make sense of challenging situations. Effective leaders ask colleagues to bring the backchannel forward so that they may validate concerns and transparently respond to rumors. In doing so, they synchronize the thinking and the responses of the organization.

Amplify Mission and Values

Effective leaders see crisis as an opportunity to amplify the mission and values of their organization in order to inspire colleagues to find meaning in their work. Effective leaders leverage mission and values as they make difficult decisions and as they communicate their response during crisis.

Celebrate People and Accomplishments

During crisis, effective leaders are both listeners and amplifiers. They monitor their surroundings for stories of accomplishment. They bring the heroics of the frontline to the fore as they highlight the inspired actions of colleagues. And in doing so they champion a narrative of efficacy that motivates their organization to move forward in adversity.

Recognize the Human Impact

Effective leaders weigh the impact of their decisions on both the short-term and long-term well-being and engagement of their colleagues and customers. They recognize and work to prevent and address burnout and seek to build resilience during difficult times.[16]

Complex Decisions

Now let's consider the more common and less time-pressured VUCA domain of complexity.

As a leader, you are familiar with complex challenges:

- How do you bring two key teams together when there is significant disagreement?
- How do you adapt your workforce to emerging fluctuations in seasonal demand?
- How do you deal with unexpected financial constraints?
- How do you respond to the emergence of an influential competitor in your market?
- How do you react to an unexpected and sweeping regulatory change?
- How do you incorporate a new technology into organizational workflow?
- What is your organizational strategy for next year?

Each of these decisions involves an interplay of various VUCA forces. Yet you have time to consider each situation in a more thoughtful manner. In the domain of complexity, leaders have time to collect the various perspectives of colleagues inside and outside of the organization before determining options and, finally, choosing a way forward to action.

When facing a complex challenge, our most effective leaders learn to switch off their expertise. They fight their urge to make reflexive decisions in the moment. And they move away from the role of individual decider toward the role of a facilitator. In the role of a leader and facilitator, they seek to leverage the collective wisdom of colleagues. They challenge their colleagues and themselves to fill in gaps and blind spots before moving to action.

NOW WHAT?

What are three VUCA decisions you face right now?

Do you sense they are in the domain of complexity or chaos?

Confused Decisions

You'll recall Blue Earth Healthy Living Clinic, the primary care physician group in turmoil after their executive team decided to open the clinic an hour earlier each morning. The executive team is struggling to accommodate increasing numbers of patients while quelling the frustration of colleagues. As they discuss how to respond, each individual on the executive team approaches the challenge from a different decision domain.

One member of the executive team wants to hire an expert consultant and have them prescribe a solution. She thinks the challenge is complicated.

Another physician executive worries they will lose valuable physicians to their competition and burn out those who stay. She wants to better understand the various perspectives of the physicians within the group. She wants to develop a sense of shared reality before considering options for how to proceed. She sees the challenge as complex.

And yet another executive wants to simply move forward without any further input and rely on the decision process the executive team has always used. Does he see the executive team as the expert? If that's the case, he sees the decision as complicated. Or does he think that they are following a commonsense best practice of leadership that the others—who are not leaders—would not understand and that the team's approach is clear? Regardless, he thinks the talk of burnout and threats of physicians leaving the practice are overblown.

It's as if each colleague stands in a different world. Together they are in the domain of confusion. They can't even agree upon the decision process.

As the managing partner of the group, Justin knows he needs to bring the leadership team together around a decision process. He appreciates how the Cynefin framework provides a common structure and language for the decision. With Justin's encouragement, the executive team considers the framework.

After spirited discussion, the team decides to approach the challenge from the complex domain. They cite VUCA-like changes in technologies, contracting, and staffing models within primary care. They note the fundamental differences of opinion they hold both on what perspectives to consider and on the possible outcomes of the decisions. They acknowledge that this wasn't a chaotic —and therefore urgently addressed—challenge. They have time to consider how to best accommodate patient needs. So they agree to further inquire, document, and share the perspectives of their colleagues before moving to action. They hold off on expanding clinic hours and consider how the information within the shared perspectives would inform their approach.

While Justin has course-corrected the group toward a more inclusive decision process, it will take time for him to earn back the trust of those colleagues who felt slighted by the executive team's initial approach.

NOW WHAT?

Think of the decisions you are making right now with colleagues.

Which of these decisions seems to be confused? Do you and your colleagues each seem to have a different impression of which decision domain applies?

How might you help your colleagues understand the different domains of decision-making?

Write down a plan for how to approach the decision in a different manner.

Leading in All Decision Domains

At any given time, a leader may oversee decisions in all domains.

For example, consider a business attempting to navigate through the crisis of COVID-19:

- An emergent virus suddenly sickens 35 percent of their workforce (chaos) . . .
- while they are considering how to respond to a competitor (complex) . . .
- as they ask their regulatory group how to remain compliant with legal aspects (complicated) . . .
- And as the workplace continues to provide healthcare benefits in the usual predictable manner (clear).

There are times when the environment is less subject to VUCA, and the steady state of expertise and best practice may be more liberally applied. And there are other times when VUCA environments dominate. An effective leader recognizes how to weave in and out of these challenges to apply the best decision-making strategy for each situation and challenge.

Leaders need to adapt to the decision-making domain. I have seen leaders rise to the challenge of emergent decisions in chaos, direct their colleagues, and lead through crisis, but then fail to adjust to the more facilitative demands of complex challenges. They continue to act like a commander when a more inclusive style of decision-making is needed. I have also seen leaders overplay their facilitative and inclusive approach during times of chaos in which they just need to make a decision. An effective leader acknowledges and adapts to the transition between the decision-making approaches needed in each domain.

NOW WHAT?

Imagine how you might structure your meetings if you identified the decision domain for each topic being discussed.

How might it change your agenda?

How might it change the effectiveness and efficiency of your meetings?

How might it enhance your ability to effectively lead?

What's Next?

Think of expertise as a tactic that is useful in some situations and hazardous in others. How you manage your own expertise determines the ultimate success of your decisions. The VUCA world calls for more than expertise, more than experience, more than strategic thinking. VUCA demands that you have an additional gear—one that allows you to use your wealth of knowledge without cutting off possible new options for action.

In the next chapter we will focus on how you can "step up to the balcony," peer over blind spots, challenge mindtraps, and gain a broader perspective of your environment.

Executive Summary

➤ The Cynefin framework gives decision-makers a conceptual place to stand within the decision habitat—a map—to sort the environment and the demands of the decision process.

➤ Decisions fall into one of five domains:

- Clear
- Complicated
- Complex
- Chaotic
- Confused

➤ For clear and complicated decisions, the cause and effects are discoverable, and the outcomes are probable. These decisions reside within the realm of the predictable world.

➤ Clear decisions are easy. When you make clear decisions, it is obvious to both you and your colleagues what is likely to happen. Clear decisions may involve single steps or multiple steps and may include best practices.

➤ Clarity depends on context; best practices may become outdated; and we get blinded by our own entrained thinking.

➤ Complicated decisions require expertise. But experts may get trapped by entrained thinking and overanalyze situations to the point of decision paralysis.

➤ When unknowable forces are at play; the data is incomplete; and the probable outcome isn't assured despite the benefits of expertise, you are likely in the unpredictable domains of complexity or chaos. These domains reside in the volatile, uncertain, complex, and ambiguous (VUCA) world.

➤ Amid chaos, there is a time crunch, and leaders need to use their experience and expertise to make quick decisions with little input in order to stop destructive forces.

➤ As effective leaders apply their decisions during the crisis of chaos, they test the environment and its response to their actions. While some aspects of the environment will remain murky and unknowable, other aspects will begin to reveal areas of order and clarity.

➤ During the times of chaos, effective leaders act with urgency, leverage their leadership team, delegate decisions, admit vulnerability, liberate time for deliberate focus, transparently communicate, bring the backchannel forward, amplify mission and values, celebrate people and accomplishments, and recognize the human impact of crisis.

➤ Complexity requires a process that leverages the collective expertise and sense-making of those inside and outside of the room. Effective leaders move away from the role of individual decider toward the role of facilitator.

➤ When colleagues cannot agree upon the decision domain, they are in the domain of confusion.

➤ At any given time, a leader may oversee decisions in all domains. An effective leader acknowledges and adapts to the transition of decision-making approaches needed in each domain.

3

STEP UP TO THE BALCONY

Our most effective leaders share stories, metaphors, and art to communicate complex ideas. Such sharing increases the contagiousness of important concepts, promotes organizational values, and unites colleagues to achieve organizational mission.

In this chapter you'll learn about a rhinoceros artist's blind spots and will be introduced to stories and drawings of mindtraps to illustrate cognitive biases. You'll gain the metaphor of the dance floor and the balcony to help you remember to pause and reflect to gain perspective.

The Rhino Artist

My favorite cartoon depicts a rhinoceros artist.

6/19   ©2017 Scott Hilburn/Distributed by Andrews McMeel Syndication

The rhinoceros stands studiously before its canvas as it paints an elephant lying joyfully in repose. The pensive artist has meticulously captured the essence of its smiling subject, except for one detail—a large rhino horn obscures much of the portrait.

As we look to the wall of the artist's studio, we notice that the rhino has painted several beautiful scenes—a river observed by clouds above, a country house, and a fruit bowl—and in every one, a big rhino horn sits smack dab in the center of the canvas.

The rhino, so diligent with its representation of the complex world, doesn't realize that it has painted itself into each painting. It doesn't perceive itself as an object separate from the scene it has painted.

Each of us has our own perspective. And ironically, each of us is subject to our own versions of a big rhino horn—our own perspectives—that eclipse our interpretation of the world.

The Problems with Your Perspective

Having viewed the rhino's dramatic blind spot, consider your own perception of reality. You reflexively lean on cognitive biases that distort your assessment of the world. This muddles your decision-making. But, thankfully, there is hope for you yet.

In the first few chapters, you learned to recognize the limits of your expertise, map the different kinds of decisions, and determine how to approach each decision domain. Now you'll learn about mindtraps—the *big rhino horns* of your thinking; the biases that shape your view of the world. Then you'll learn how to reset or reposition your perspective—to step off the dance floor and step up to the balcony—during moments of decision to find greater clarity and see around some of your biases.

Mindtraps

In her insightful book *Unlocking Leadership Mindtraps*, Jennifer Garvey Berger described five reflexive shortcuts that leaders commonly take as they think about complex issues.[1] She calls these shortcuts "mindtraps," each one leading to the creation of blind spots—the *big rhino horns* of our thinking. According to Garvey Berger, we are trapped by:

1. Simple stories

2. Rightness

3. Agreement

4. Control

5. Ego

Simple Stories

If you and I were to stand in the backyard of my Minnesota home during a crisp, cloudless winter night, we'd look up at the sky and see a sea of stars. We'd gaze upon the array of shining dots and recognize constellations, groups of stars that tell a story. Perhaps you would look up toward the south and see Orion, the hunter of the night sky, with his broad shoulders, belt, and knife clearly visible. Or in the northern sky you might see Perseus, the Greek hero who slayed the Gorgon Medusa. You'd find Mirfak and Algol, the two brightest stars, and that would lead you to the center of the constellation. Whereas I . . . I would most likely look up, with my senescent eyes, and see a chicken taco and a beer, accompanied by a group of stars resembling an antacid—constellation Heartburn.

Each of us looks at the same sky. Each of us connects the dots. Yet each of us authors a different story about the sky. We parse data and construct a narrative that translates our perceptions of the complex environment.

We may start out with the same disparate facts, but our brains quickly generate stories to fill in the blanks. You may hear that someone was fired. But your brain won't stop there. You'll swing into simple story mode: "Oh, I believe that. It's probably because of the constant budget overruns in his department. No wonder they finally lowered the boom on him. That spending spree couldn't go on forever." Or perhaps you hear about someone who was hired. "Well, that makes sense since she and the department head used to work together at a previous job." You didn't actually learn more about either of those two employment situations. You took the random facts and fashioned a story out of them. In that way, the information you received feels less random.

Solomon Asch, a pioneer in social psychology, examined how our initial impressions of someone are shaped by the order of information we receive about them.[2]

Consider these two potential job candidates. Who would you be more likely to hire, Tami or Diane?

Tami: intelligent, industrious, impulsive, critical, stubborn,
   envious

Diane: envious, stubborn, critical, impulsive, industrious
   intelligent

Tami and Diane have the same traits written in different order. However, Asch's research suggests that people would form a more favorable impression of Tami at first glance.

Think of how your emotional and physical states affect the stories you construct. Imagine how your story unfolds when you're happy and well-rested versus when you are tired and insecure. How about the moment after you receive a positive comment from a colleague versus the time when your other colleague expressed their fear and disagreement? How do you think when you're hungry?

Then consider what you have just read on social media, the explanatory theories recently promoted by your social group, and the way you translate the intentions of others who hold opposing viewpoints.

And finally, layer in your gender identity, your ethnicity, your race, your economic status, your political points of view, your favorite sports team, and consider how each of these elements are reflected in the narratives you construct as you make sense of the world.

We can fashion a simple story about anything in the moment.

We consume data and we construct stories to explain our perceptions. Often, we are so confident about these stories that we don't
even perceive a possibility that parts of our stories might be works of
free-form creative nonfiction—including elements of fiction based
upon a true story. But from the perspective of others—individuals
with different beliefs and experiences—our stories may appear to be
works of pure fiction. And given the same information, their charac-
ters and the plot appear to be quite different to us.

NOW WHAT?

Write about a time when you were certain, but later found that you had
missed key details and different perspectives. What simple stories were
you creating in that moment?

Name five groups you align with that may affect the simple stories you
tell yourself. Consider social, religious, political, organizational, and professional groups.

Rightness

Recall, from the beginning of the book, the leader at the meeting
who concluded that "you are all incorrect, and we will proceed with
my plan." But participants at meetings often do this as well. As we
hear others speak, we think "yes, you are correct, I agree with you,"
"nope, you are incorrect, please stop talking," and "I can talk to them
after the meeting to help them see my way." We tend to feel most
comfortable when we think we are right. We tend to defend our
rightness. And if you try to argue this point with me, I guarantee
you, I will disagree.

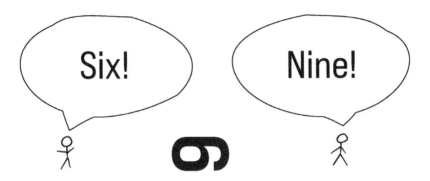

Not being right—being wrong—causes physical discomfort for many of us. Many of the executives I coach describe how their chest tightens, their heart races, their palms sweat, and they clam up or speak with a pressured voice when the views of others conflict with their own. They relay a sense of feeling defensive, annoyed, and offended. They view these moments as personal failures. They would prefer to remain open and curious and to be less captured by emotion.

Many of us consider ourselves to be receptive to other points of view. We want to be challenged. Yet when we hear those different perspectives, we filter them through our current thinking—which often is based upon the simple stories we have constructed. "I've thought about that already. That is not valid. Because of this, this, and this." Yet in the complex world, what we discount as irrelevant, as not being pertinent to our situation, may be quite relevant, or in fact pivotal in the broader scheme. Things change. And when we gaze at the world within the comfort of tunnel vision, we don't perceive change. We sense we are correct; we sense we are right. We remain right in our own head, right behind our blind spots.

Agreement

The people of Minnesota have a reputation for being polite and friendly. They're generally agreeable and avoid standing out or appearing confrontational. They are "Minnesota nice."

Being around people who are "Minnesota nice" has its benefits. There are lots of smiles and hellos when you go for a walk or check-out at the grocery store. People tend to go out of their way to help each other. Minnesota is genuinely a pleasant place to live.

However, "Minnesota nice" has its dark side. There are times when a colleague flashes a neighborly smile and gives an affirmative nod even when they disagree. You think they agree, but they don't feel comfortable revealing disagreement. Thus, important differences of opinion and alternative perspectives can be withheld, albeit politely.

"Whatever you do, don't rock the boat. Be agreeable." This is a belief that many individuals—both inside and outside of Minnesota—hold. Yes, when we face complexity, we need friendly, respectful, and cooperative interactions. But we also need to share diverse perspectives to overcome complex challenges.

We may sense that disagreement creates confrontation, so instead we choose to compromise. We make concessions in our thinking and about what might be possible. We remain quiet and withhold alternative perspectives and options so that we do not appear (or feel) hostile, rather than accepting the discomfort of collaboration.

It might be hard to disagree. Perhaps you do not feel safe disagreeing. You might fear that you will lose a friend, alienate a colleague, or anger an individual in a position of power. Perhaps your 360 review is coming up and you don't want to quash your chances of getting promoted. You don't want to be scored as disagreeable—as not being a team player. Perhaps it is inconvenient, the meeting is already running long, and if you offer a different perspective, you will keep others from their lunch. So you stay quiet, or flash a faint smile, and move on.

NOW WHAT?

List specific situations in which you have withheld your thoughts and then later wished you had spoken up. What was it about the situation that kept you quiet?

Control

We'd like to think we are in control. And as we learned from the Cynefin framework in Chapter Two, when we encounter either clear or complicated issues, we still have significant control over how our actions influence the predictable environment. But we also learned that our control over the environment dissipates as we encounter unpredictable challenges.

When facing complexity, we tend to overestimate the effectiveness of our personal power. We errantly tell ourselves that we can mastermind a step-by-step strategy. We view colleagues and resources as chess pieces, and we plot the right moves given our simple stories. We try to control the environment to produce our desired outcome. But such an approach lacks self-control.

Paul Nutt, a professor of management sciences at The Ohio State University, found that when leaders make strategic decisions using the controls of edict and persuasion, half of those decisions fail.[3] Yet when a leader releases their tight grip on the decision-making process—to involve others, to search for understanding, to generate multiple ideas and options, to understand implementation, and to identify barriers—the likelihood of success in the complex environment increases.

We seek opportunities to use our expertise and experience to pave specific paths. We prefer to identify precise actions under our direct control as we plot our route to our desired destination. But in the VUCA space, there are many unknowns, and as the map evolves, there is no way to control this space.

Ego

In my coaching practice, leaders have expressed the following assumptions:

- My success comes from my ability to control the narrative.
- My power and authority come from making people get the job done.
- I need to micromanage; otherwise, things will not get done.
- A lack of success is a lack of will.
- I will lose the respect of my colleagues if they see that I don't know what to do.

Each assumption is rooted in the leader's ego. Their sense of who they are and their efficacy in the world is premised on protecting their current impression of themselves.

As you and I read the above assumptions, some of them perhaps sound hyperbolic, while others may sound quite reasonable. On the outside looking in, we can see that some of these beliefs seem exaggerated. We may know, and indeed each individual leader may sense, that a lack of success on a specific project does not necessarily signal a problem with our leadership, our ability, our delegation, and so on. But at the same time, such a notion can be hard to shake.

In their *Harvard Business Review* article "The Real Reason People Won't Change," Robert Kegan and Lisa Lahey describe how limiting assumptions often develop early in life but are seldom critically examined when applied many years later.[4] Each leader has a soundtrack of limiting assumptions, whether conscious or unconscious, that plays in their head as they perceive the world. These assumptions about themselves and the world around them both inform and distort the way they interpret and respond to challenges. The soundtrack of limiting assumptions plays, even when situations are quite different, and those assumptions guide a reflexive and maladaptive response that is out of rhythm with effective leadership. They preserve the ego in the moment, but they rely on an impression of self that is shackled by past experience.[5]

In Chapter Ten, we will explore the effect of limiting assumptions and examine the validity of these ego-entwined hypotheses.

Step Up to the Balcony

Like the rhino artist, each of us has significant blind spots in our framing of reality. We are trapped within the biases of our simple stories, our need to be right, our seeking of agreement, our sense of control, and our ego. But with deliberate practice and process we can broaden our perspective, helping ourselves and those we lead to see past blind spots.

In *Leadership Without Easy Answers*, Ronald Heifetz, a senior lecturer at Harvard's Kennedy School of Government, writes of leadership as both active and reflective.[6] He urges leaders to alternate between participating and observing. To illustrate his point, he introduces us to the metaphor of the dance floor and the balcony.

Imagine your organization as a dance floor. You attend meetings, you read memos and reports, and you interact with colleagues.

You perceive the environment and you respond. Sometimes you are in sync; at other times you are not.

Dance Floor

On the dance floor, you and your colleagues are immersed in thoughts, in emotions, and in the dynamics of an immediate ever-evolving situation. Your expertise guides you, and you react in the moment. At times this serves you well; at other times, not so much. You see those dancing nearest to you, sense how they think and feel, and you respond. However, your perspective from the dance floor is limited.

Then, seeking to broaden your perspective, you look above the dance floor and notice a balcony. When you step up to the balcony, you gaze down upon the dance floor. Now you can focus on the elements of the dance floor that you were unable to see while enmeshed with others in your reactive experience. And as you move away from the pressures and the rhythm of real-time response, you have an opportunity to consider alternate points of view.

The balcony perspective nurtures insight. It isn't so distant as to provide a 30,000-foot airplane view, where you're disconnected from people and organizations, and everything is a blur of nebulous geographic patterns. No, here you are still connected to reality. And as

Balcony

Dance Floor

you observe your environment, you see specifics, you see individuals, and you leverage different perspectives to understand the complexity of real-world reality. You can take it all in and make sense of your environment with a more expansive view. You can peer over blind spots.

Let's be clear that you go to the balcony to gain perspective, not to be seen by others.[7] It is neither a perch from which to manage others nor a roost from which to shout orders. You go to the balcony to think, not to do. The time for generating options and taking action occurs later.

What's Next?

In the rest of this book you'll learn processes for stepping up onto the balcony. You'll learn how to conduct one-to-one conversations that help colleagues look over blind spots and make sense of their complex challenges. You'll bring large groups of colleagues up to the balcony to consider and define your collective approach to thorny and unpredictable situations.

The next chapter focuses on developing a balcony perspective of burnout and well-being. When colleagues are burned out, they are emotionally exhausted, cynical, and less effective. When we lead to promote engagement and well-being, we improve the effectiveness of our colleagues and organizations.

Executive Summary

➤ Each of us has blind spots in our perspective of the world.

➤ Five mindtraps propagate those blind spots: we create simple stories, we need to be right, we seek agreement, we need to feel in control, and we protect our ego.

➤ We create simple stories to explain the complex environment based upon our own experience, physical and mental state, expertise, identity, and beliefs.

➤ We filter what we hear based upon a need to be right. We seek to support our current thinking.

➤ We seek agreement and see disagreement as being confrontational. As a result, we compromise, rather than collaborate.

➤ We aim to control situations. We think that we can leverage our expertise and experience to plot a specific path with prescribed actions to persuade outcomes even in complex environments.

➤ We protect our identity and our current impression of ourselves; we protect our ego.

➤ Reinforcing these mindtraps, we hold limiting assumptions about ourselves. These are deeply rooted beliefs that shackle our egos to our interpretations of past experiences and decrease our effectiveness as leaders today.

STEP UP TO THE BALCONY   75

➤ Leaders must alternate between participating and observing, as in the metaphor of the dance floor and the balcony. Leaders need to spend time on the balcony away from the pressures and the rhythm of real-time response of the dance floor. The balcony perspective nurtures insight as it provides an opportunity to look over blind spots and make sense of the environment with a more expansive view.

4

UNDERSTAND BURNOUT
AND WELL-BEING

Each year I give a presentation about burnout and well-being to our recently hired physicians and scientists at Mayo Clinic. During the talk, I ask the participants to raise their hand if they have ever experienced burnout. Five years ago, a few hands would go up. Today, in 2022, nearly everyone in the room raises their hand.

Did the rate of burnout for these professionals increase significantly over the past five years? Perhaps, especially recently with the pandemic. Alternatively, we may simply be better at recognizing burnout. We have become more familiar with the language that defines burnout and the metrics that quantify it—so now we can name what we perceive.[1] And if we as leaders aim to decrease burnout, having a framework to identify and figure out how to approach burnout and well-being is essential.

While conducting a recent seminar with leaders of healthcare organizations throughout Asia and the Middle East, I likewise asked the participants, "How many of you have experienced burnout?" Every one of the people, at tables assembled by organization and country, raised their hand—except for the individuals at one table.

I thought to myself, "Finally, an organization has figured out how to eliminate burnout." So I asked those at the table to share their experience.

Each leader at the table looked sullenly at the others. Eventually one of them grabbed the microphone and stood up to speak. "Each of us in our country has experienced difficult childhoods with much adversity. We learned at a young age that the way to succeed was to put our head down and work as hard and as many hours as we could. And we expect this of each other. Certainly, we face adversity. There are times when we feel sad and helpless, but we need to push through these moments." He looked down and switched the microphone to the opposite hand. "Many of my colleagues who have retired from work reflect negatively upon their lives. They realized that the moments of sadness and helplessness they experienced turned into a career of misery. They tell me that they sense that they had never experienced joy. They regret the life they have lived." He then looked directly at me. "But we do not label our experience as burnout."

What Is Burnout?

Burnout is a syndrome of overwhelming emotional exhaustion, feelings of cynicism, and a sense of ineffectiveness.[2]

Emotional exhaustion occurs when we are worn out, fatigued, depleted, and without emotional energy. It creates a cognitive weariness that affects our ability to perform our work. A candle requires sufficient oxygen, protection from the wind, and a spark to keep its wax burning; lacking those conditions, it would lose its capacity to make light and heat. Similarly, our vigor is extinguished when we are emotionally exhausted.[3]

Cynicism refers to the negative attitudes that develop when we encounter our work. When we are cynical, we become irritable and lose our idealism. We begin to see colleagues and clients as obstacles in our way.

When I think of cynicism, I am reminded of the cartoon character Glum from *The Adventures of Gulliver*.[4] When Glum and his friends faced a difficult challenge, Glum would proclaim, "We'll never make it!" Glum's friends would counter, "Be positive, Glum." And then after a few moments Glum would admonish, "I'm *positive* we'll never make it!"

A colleague is clinically burned out when they have high levels of emotional exhaustion in addition to cynicism or a sense of ineffectiveness.[5] All of us have moments in which we experience each of these feelings. But it is the combination of relentless exhaustion over time and at least one of the other two dimensions that separates burnout from simple exhaustion.[6]

What Causes Burnout?

You likely have a good idea of what promotes burnout. Imagine:

- Your inbox is full of "high priority" messages, a work schedule change bumps a long-planned family gathering, and you're denied an essential resource because you submitted the wrong form.
- Your boss overlooks your input on a decision within your area of expertise, your colleague barks at you each time you follow his instructions to contact him, and you were just given another important project with poorly defined deliverables on an unrealistically tight deadline.
- The mission and values of your organization seem to exist only on the screen savers of your workstation—the workstation which, as it happens, suddenly restarts whenever you open the HR portal to complete a required questionnaire about burnout.
- You haven't had a vacation, you haven't been eating well, and you don't have time to sleep. And, in the back of your mind— what wakes you up at 3 a.m. each day—is a perseverative

thought about a mistake you made last month. You feel as if you are treading water in a pool with no ladder and a poolside edge that lurks six feet above the water's surface.

And it doesn't appear these struggles will ever end.

Burnout

Emotional Exhaustion
Cynicism
Decreased Effectiveness

Each of us has the grit to work through process inefficiencies, and excessive workloads, and work and home conflicts, and dysfunction within our organizations.[7, 8] We are resilient and can bounce back after struggles or failure. We may even consider exhaustion to be a badge of honor—proof of our dedication to work—as we speak with pride of the sacrifices we make in service of our pursuits.[9] We face moments of frustration and we persevere. But when these moments repeat, and are unrelenting, and we have no time for recovery over longer periods of time, we are at risk of developing burnout.

Why Burnout Matters

My assumption in writing this book is that you are a well-meaning, virtuous individual who wants in some way to make the world a better place through your leadership. But perhaps this is not the case. Perhaps you're more like a villainous business mogul, viewing the souls of your minions as kindling to fuel your evil master plan. First, thank you for purchasing this book. Second, unfortunately for you, burnout still matters—it reduces the organization's effectiveness.

Not only does burnout incur devastating personal costs—with an associated increase in depression, anxiety, suicide, broken relationships, and alcohol and substance use—but burnout also damages an organization's ability to function effectively. Burnout is associated with an increase in errors, decrease in productivity, increase in employee turnover, and decrease in customer satisfaction.[10]

Burnout injures the individual, the organization, and our ability to serve others. While the causes of burnout are complex, effective leaders can reduce the incidence of burnout in their colleagues.

NOW WHAT?

Have you experienced burnout?

What was it about the situation in your life at the time that contributed to a sense of burnout?

Well-Being

Just as a leader must understand burnout, it is important to also understand well-being. And as we recognize the factors that contribute to well-being, we may identify the actions we can take to enhance well-being. We note the specific things we do that either enhance or detract from our well-being. We become attuned to the productive and destructive behaviors of others. But first, we need to be able to describe what we perceive.

When I was a child and felt ill, I would go to my mother and say, "My tummy hurts." And she would respond, "Oh, that sounds uncomfortable."

Now that I'm older, having completed medical school, my vocabulary has become much more anatomically specific. Now, when I feel ill, I call my mother and say, "I think there is something wrong with my sigmoid colon or perhaps my left psoas muscle." And she responds, "Oh, that sounds uncomfortable."

The point is not to highlight my abdominal ailments, but to emphasize the importance of developing a language and structure for thinking about what was going on inside of me. In this case, what used to be my "tummy" transformed into a complicated system of organs and body parts—each with its own name, function, and potential for pathology and health. As I expanded my language, I could more accurately identify and describe what might occur inside of me.

When I give the burnout and well-being talk to Mayo Clinic's newly hired physicians and scientists, I like to quiz them with another series of questions.

I ask, "How many of you can name six causes of metabolic acidosis?" And almost everyone in the room raises their hand.

"How many of you can name the twelve cranial nerves?" Again, most of my colleagues raise a hand.

"How many of you can name the six components of psychological well-being?" No hands are raised. I get blank stares.

These are individuals who can name almost every aspect of human physiology, anatomy, and pathology, who know the human condition inside and out, yet they don't have names for the dimensions of psychology that promote their own well-being.

Six Dimensions of Psychological Well-Being

According to Carol Ryff, a psychologist at the University of Wisconsin–Madison, psychological well-being is composed of six dimensions:[11]

> **Purpose.** We sense that we can achieve our goals in a manner that aligns with our values and beliefs. This helps give our life meaning.
>
> **Autonomy.** We sense that we are self-determining and can speak up with our own independent voice to be heard. We can resist social pressures that would have us think or act in an incongruous manner.
>
> **Personal Growth.** We sense that we are learning, gaining new experience, and reaching our potential. We continue to develop and improve our effectiveness.
>
> **Environmental Mastery.** We sense that we can manage and control our environment. We have the tools and resources needed to fulfill our capability.
>
> **Positive Relations with Others.** We sense that we have warm, satisfying, and trusting relationships with others. We sense the give and take, and the compromises needed to sustain healthy relationships.
>
> **Self-Acceptance.** We maintain a positive attitude toward self with an acceptance of both our best qualities and our personal mistakes, quirks, and challenges.

Psychological Well-Being

Purpose
Autonomy
personal Growth
Environmental mastery
positive Relations with others
Self-acceptance

The psychological well-being scale gives a leader a framework that names six specific dimensions that promote fulfillment in life and work. An effective leader who wishes to promote well-being will maintain alignment with organizational mission and values; encourage individuals to speak their minds; maximize potential and nurture opportunities for learning; secure needed resources; promote a climate of positive interpersonal interactions; and model the acceptance of both success and failure.

An ineffective leader, on the other hand, will oversee an uncoordinated deviation from mission and values; silence independent voices; commodify individuals in their current state; withhold needed resources; isolate colleagues and encourage altercation; and reprimand failure. They will decrease well-being and maximize burnout.

Levels of Efficacy

When we are burned out, we perceive our experience in dichotomies, us versus them, or me versus the rest of the world. That limits our power to make necessary changes in our environment.

Alternatively, we can examine the space between ourselves and the rest of the world; the space inhabited by our organization, our individual thoughts and behaviors, and our interpersonal interactions. It is within the different levels of this more local space where we find efficacy. At each level, there are actions we may take to help lead ourselves and our colleagues away from burnout and toward well-being.

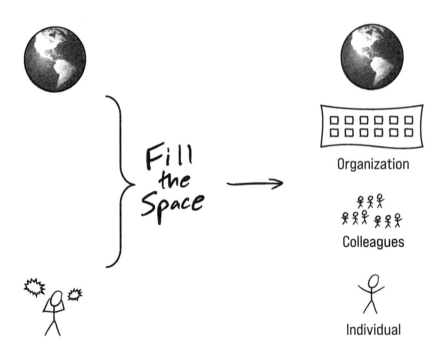

The Individual Level

If you have thirty-seven priority emails you need to answer, your coworkers snap at you, your boss sets an unattainable deadline for your already short-handed team, your organizational culture ferments like an old, expired cup of yogurt, and you feel burned out—you need to meditate.

So, you meditate. Then, when you go back to work the next day in the same environment and you still feel burned out, you think to yourself, "I must not know how to meditate correctly." So, you schedule a meditation course, and, in the meantime, you go for a run.

And then, despite going for a run, you still feel emotionally exhausted and cynical. So, you eat fewer processed foods and focus on getting enough sleep. But even then, after weeks of a daily practice of meditation, exercise, healthy eating, and adequate sleep, you still feel burned out.

Perhaps at that moment you have an epiphany. You realize that your sense of well-being also involves—is intertwined with—your experience in the work environment. It's hard to be meditative when you are being poked. It's hard to align with organizational values if you are being fed sour culture. Your sense of purpose, autonomy, personal growth, environmental mastery, positive relations, and self-acceptance has two parts to it: your internal world (which you can work on) and the external world (which you and others can work on together). If you don't attend to both the internal and external world, your potential to move away from burnout toward well-being will be diminished.

Consider how you might optimize your psychological and physical well-being—your internal environment. Meditation, exercise, sleeping well, and eating whole foods—all of these can greatly improve your resilience and your experience of the world. Are you as effective after sleeping too little, eating poorly, and perseverating on issues? No. Might you be more likely to become emotionally exhausted, cynical, and less effective in such a depleted state? Yes.

Imagine that you and I decide that we will run a marathon two months from now. We want to be well-prepared, so we further decide that after we finish reading this chapter we will put on our running shoes and then run continuously for the two months leading up to the race. The farther and the faster we run, we estimate, the more prepared we will become.

Brad Stulberg and Steve Magness coach elite athletes, executives, and entrepreneurs. In their book *Peak Performance*, they write about the growth equation: Stress + Rest = Growth.[13] This equation works for the elite athlete, but it also works for leaders. Our passion and drive to achieve must be paired with periods of rest and recovery. Athletes experience decreased performance and increased rates of injury if intensive workouts are not balanced with periods of recovery. Like athletes, thinkers must also pair times of deep focus with periods of recovery to promote the emergence of insight.[14] Without recovery, our efforts to excel build upon a rickety foundation that eventually collapses under stress. It is during periods of rest and recovery that our efforts consolidate and strengthen a framework that promotes growth.

Stress + Rest = Growth

Many of us have an insatiable appetite for achievement. We want to do more, we want to be better, and we want to be faster. This is certainly the case for many of the successful professionals and executives whom I coach: the executive who wants to rocket through the formal leadership ranks to be vice president, the scientist who wants to publish a lifetime's worth of manuscripts and achieve professorship in a short amount of time, and the professional who seeks perfection. But these drives are often built upon our fears, worries, and assumptions about what might happen as we navigate the complex world.

When we are driven by a fear of missing out, or of being left behind, or of losing something, we risk becoming cruel, unrelenting taskmasters engaged in an unforgiving internal dialogue with ourselves about ourselves.

Seth Godin, an educator and entrepreneur, wrote about the world's worst boss—the voice inside our own head:

> If you had a manager that talked to you the way you talked to you, you'd quit. If you had a boss that wasted as much of your time as you do, they'd fire her. If an organization developed its employees as poorly as you are developing yourself, it would soon go under.[15]

Sometimes the world's worst boss, the uncomfortable and perseverative voice inside our own head, becomes the voice we use as we speak to colleagues. If we don't pay attention, this voice of dysfunctional drive and passion contributes to the burnout of those we lead.

The Organizational Level

Burnout and well-being are neither the sole responsibility of the leader nor the sole responsibility of the individual. Achieving the goals of decreased burnout and increased well-being is the shared responsibility of both the individual and the organization. This shared responsibility includes the organization's board of directors and everyone in positions of leadership.[16, 17]

It is difficult to influence rates of burnout—and to share responsibility for its occurrence—if you don't measure it. You need data. Just as organizations evaluate measures of productivity, quality, and cost, measures of burnout must be tracked. Quantitative and qualitative data provide information about the organization as a whole, its workgroups, and each individual. The results promote debate and conversations to understand what was measured (and not measured), and then what to do about it. More on this later in the book as we discuss the ROW Forward framework.

A note to organizations: individual data about burnout and well-being is personal. While you should encourage individuals to understand their own level of burnout and well-being, the results for each individual should be kept confidential and known only by the individual measured. This ensures not just privacy but also a more authentic response to inquiries.

Within healthcare, there is a concept known as "The Triple Aim."[18] The Triple Aim of an organization is to improve the health of a population of patients (Aim 1) with a high level of patient experience (Aim 2) at a lower per capita cost (Aim 3). Other industries have similar goals: improve the quality of your product or service, improve the level of customer satisfaction, and do so at a lower overall cost. But what if while achieving the Triple Aim, you do so at the expense of the well-being of your colleagues, your employees, or in the case of Mr. Villainous Business Mogul, your minions? Such an approach would fail over time. Staff turnover would rise, errors would increase, and productivity would fall.

So in medicine we now focus on "The Quadruple Aim," which combines the measures of the Triple Aim with measures of staff burnout and well-being.[19] The individuals, the humans, who generate your product and services need to be nurtured and maintained to operate effectively.

Measure Well-Being and Burnout

Many organizations use all-staff surveys to measure the rates of burnout and well-being. Some organizations survey their staff annually, while others do so at more frequent intervals. But what if your organization doesn't distribute an all-staff survey? You could still decide to survey your work unit.

The Maslach Burnout Inventory (MBI)—a twenty-two-item questionnaire—is commonly used to measure burnout.[20] There are many other validated measures of burnout based on Maslach's work, some consisting of as few as two questions.[21]

There are many validated survey instruments that measure dimensions of employee well-being. Questions on such surveys generally parallel dimensions of Ryff's psychological well-being scale cited earlier. It is common to ask respondents to rank their agreement with a survey question on a numerical scale. For example, from 1 (strongly disagree) to 7 (strongly agree) rank your impression of the following statements:

- "My work environment makes it easy to live up to organizational mission and values." (Purpose)
- "Where I work, I feel free to speak my mind without fear of negative consequences." (Autonomy)
- "I believe that my workplace provides opportunities for personal growth and development." (Personal Growth)
- "My workplace provides the tools and resources necessary for me to do my job." (Environmental Mastery)
- "My workplace is a place of trust, mutual respect, and collaboration." (Positive Relations)
- "I feel safe to admit and learn from my mistakes in the workplace." (Self-acceptance)

Individual responses to survey questions are kept anonymous and the results may be examined across the organization or by work unit.

But what do you do with the results of the burnout and well-being survey? For example, what if the marketing division scores high on burnout (not good) and low on well-being (also, not good) when compared to other work units?

- Do you fire the marketing director?
- Do you conclude that the department scores poorly because the marketing folks lack grit and have poor resilience?
- Or do you think the scores are a result of the marketing folks being bullied by the people in sales? Perhaps you should fire those sales leaders instead.

No. These would not be correct interpretations of the survey.

A better approach to evaluating survey results would be to first seek a deeper understanding of the underperforming well-being and burnout scores. These results represent a quantitative summary of a complex environment. Perhaps the marketing department needs more resources, perhaps external factors or cultural issues are affecting their results, and perhaps a few disruptive individuals need guidance.

When you receive the survey results, you may not know what triggered the responses, but you do know there are blind spots. You know it would be better to step up to the balcony to gain a broader perspective of the complex challenge before you take action.

The best approach is to withhold blame and seek to understand the people enduring burnout.

Burnout Myths

In closing we should specifically address some myths:

1. Burnout is the individual's fault.

Burnout is a result of the system that includes the organization, the individual, and the interpersonal interactions that occur each day. The system produces burnout, and the system can produce well-being.

2. Burnout is a terminal diagnosis.

Many of us face moments of burnout throughout our lives. During these times, we have an opportunity to stand on the balcony—both alone and with colleagues—to reconsider and to reset our behaviors and our surroundings so that we may move toward well-being.

3. Individuals are powerless victims of burnout.

Each of us has an opportunity to examine how our inner environment (the way we think and behave) and our external environment (our organization and interactions with colleagues) contribute to burnout. If we have agency—the capacity to make free choices—then we can attempt to improve our inner and external environment. There may be times when it is necessary to leave a destructive environment.

The Interpersonal Level

Throughout the rest of this book, you will learn how to approach your interpersonal interactions with colleagues. You will learn techniques that will improve your ability to have one-to-one conversations and to facilitate group decision-making. As a leader, when you rise above the blind spots within expertise, you promote a workplace that encourages value-aligned action and nurtures the best from colleagues. In the next chapter, you will learn how to amplify effective leadership behaviors that promote satisfaction and well-being.

Executive Summary

➤ Burnout is a syndrome of overwhelming emotional exhaustion combined with feelings of cynicism and/or a sense of ineffectiveness.

➤ Burnout is a result of a combination of process inefficiencies, excessive workloads, work and home conflicts, and dysfunction within our organizations.

➤ Each of us has grit. We face moments of frustration and we persevere. But when these moments repeat, and are unrelenting, and we have no time for recovery over longer periods of time, we are at risk of developing burnout.

➤ Burnout incurs both devastating personal costs—with an associated increase in depression, anxiety, suicide, broken relationships, and alcohol and substance use—and organizational costs—with an increase in errors, decreased productivity, increased turnover, and decreased customer satisfaction.

➤ There are Six Dimensions of Psychological Well-Being: purpose, autonomy, personal growth, environmental mastery, positive relations with others, and self-acceptance.

➤ An effective leader will maintain alignment with organizational mission and values, encourage individuals to speak their minds, nurture opportunities for learning and maximizing potential, secure needed resources, promote a climate of positive interpersonal interactions, and model the acceptance of both success and failure. This supports psychological well-being.

➤ There are three levels of efficacy with respect to decreasing burnout and improving well-being: individual, organizational, and interpersonal. An individual might also try to change the world. But that is more difficult.

➤ It is essential to combine times of effort with times of recovery to promote growth. Stress + Rest = Growth.

➤ Our own drive to achieve can be a factor that drives burnout.

➤ The internal fears, worries, and assumptions of a leader affect their internal state and may contribute to burnout in those they lead.

➤ Organizations must measure, track, and respond to metrics of burnout and well-being.

➤ Burnout and well-being are complex challenges.

5

AMPLIFY ENGAGEMENT

Teresa faces a complex challenge. Over the coming year, as the chief medical officer of a large healthcare system, she will champion a change in the electronic health record (EHR) system of her organization. The EHR is the operating system of healthcare: it holds patient care notes, test results, and treatment algorithms, and it makes this data instantly available to patients and care providers. This transition will alter the way her physician and nursing colleagues capture each vital sign, order each treatment, and document each episode of care. It will transform the quality management process, the billing process, and the communication process among patients, physicians, nurses, administrators, and vendors. Switching the EHR is like changing a plane's entire operating system midflight. It will occur while surgeries are taking place and as ambulances deliver critical patients through the emergency department's doors. There will be no time to pause when the new EHR "goes live." Everything needs to work well immediately.

The good news is that Teresa has a year to prepare for what will surely be a disruptive upgrade. However, she reads headlines each day that warn her of the cost overruns, job losses, and delays in patient care that other organizations unexpectedly encountered while upgrading their EHRs.[1, 2] She recently attended a conference with several professional colleagues who had migrated their organizations' EHR. These once-optimistic individuals now sounded exhausted and glum. They appeared to have aged rapidly since she last saw them.

Teresa wants to lead an effective rollout. She recognizes that the next year will be difficult, but she senses an opportunity to elevate the effectiveness of her organization, and to rally her team together around a common cause.

Yesterday, Teresa spoke with Charlotte, a mentor to whom she had reported while at a previous organization. Charlotte had recently overseen a successful EHR launch, and Teresa wanted her thoughts about the challenges ahead. As she spoke with Charlotte, Teresa had flashbacks of how wonderful it had been working with her. Their team had a palpable esprit de corps even while facing tough challenges. Charlotte had clearly been in charge, but she had a way of empowering those she worked with and coaching them to develop their talent and skills. Teresa always felt recognized and heard—even when she was not the most "expert" or "senior" individual working on an issue. Each of her teammates had functioned at the top of their games and gone on to impressive accomplishments.

As Teresa hung up the phone, she felt re-energized. Teresa wants to inspire her team as Charlotte always inspired her. She wants to help people work to be their best selves and to embrace this complex challenge. She also wants to prevent burnout—both for herself and for her colleagues during the challenging months ahead.

This chapter focuses on effective leadership behaviors. You will discover eight specific leadership behaviors that effective leaders embody to decrease burnout and increase engagement. You will learn specific actions you may adopt to more effectively develop, recognize, inform, value, engage, respect, and supervise colleagues. These behaviors matter the most when you lead a complex transformation, but they'll come in handy in every leadership situation.

Leadership Behaviors

Lotte Dyrbye, chief well-being officer for the University of Colorado School of Medicine, studied how leadership behaviors affect the satisfaction and burnout rates of employees.[3] In one study, she and her colleagues sent 57,000 Mayo Clinic employees a picture of their immediate supervisor and asked each of them to rate their boss' behavior.

Each person who answered the survey rated how well their immediate supervisor:

1. Holds career development conversations with them.
2. Empowers them to do their job.
3. Treats them with dignity and respect.
4. Provides helpful feedback and coaching on their performance.
5. Recognizes them for a job well done.
6. Keeps them informed about changes taking place at Mayo Clinic.
7. Encourages them to develop their talent and skills.
8. Encourages them to suggest ideas for improvement.

And finally, they were asked:

9. Overall, how satisfied are you with your immediate supervisor?[4]

Apparently evaluating one's boss is an enjoyable task because almost 40,000 employees clicked from 1 (very dissatisfied) to 5 (very satisfied) to anonymously reveal their impression of their boss's leadership behaviors.

Dr. Dyrbye's research found that leadership behaviors matter a lot. For every one-point increase in a dimension of leadership behavior there was an 11 percent increase in the likelihood of satisfaction and a 7 percent decrease in the likelihood of burnout within a leader's work area. This makes sense, doesn't it? Would you like to be treated with dignity and respect? Yes. Would you like to be recognized for a job well done? Yes, of course.

These questions mirror many of the key domains of well-being we explored in the previous chapter. When we encourage colleagues to develop their talent and skills and we hold career development conversations with them, we promote the personal growth dimension of psychological well-being. When we encourage individuals to suggest ideas for improvement and treat them with dignity and respect, we support autonomy and perhaps purpose. Positive relations with others is woven into each behavior.

When a leader attends to the dimensions of psychological well-being of their colleagues, they decrease burnout and increase the satisfaction of their employees. Similar research examined the effects of leadership behaviors on more than 2,800 Mayo Clinic physicians and scientists as they rated their immediate supervisor. Not even a doctorate degree could shield one from the behaviors of their boss.[5] The physicians and scientists whose leader scored high in the expression of leadership behaviors had higher rates of well-being, whereas those physicians and scientists whose leader scored lower had higher rates of burnout and lower job satisfaction.

Extensive reviews of the leadership literature reinforce the concept that a leader can be either a buffer from stress at work or an enabler of it.[6] Which leader would you rather work with: the leader who develops, recognizes, informs, values, and engages you, or the one who does not?

NOW WHAT?

How well do you think you would score if your colleagues were to rate your leadership behaviors?

How would you self-rate your leadership behaviors on a scale from 1 (very dissatisfied) to 5 (very satisfied)?

1. I hold career development conversations with my direct reports.
2. I empower my direct reports to do their job.
3. I treat my direct reports with dignity and respect.
4. I provide helpful feedback and coaching to my direct reports on their performance.
5. I recognize my direct reports for a job well done.
6. I keep my direct reports informed about changes taking place at our organization.
7. I encourage my direct reports to develop their talent and skills.
8. I encourage my direct reports to suggest ideas for improvement.
9. Overall, how satisfied do I think my direct reports are with my leadership?

Which behaviors are your strongest?

Which of the behaviors should you focus on improving?

The DRIVERS of Engagement

Many leaders *think* about engaging their colleagues. Thinking is good, but thoughts need to result in specific actions. Our most effective leaders embody the specific leadership behaviors that result in the engagement of colleagues. These leaders develop, recognize, inspire, value, engage, respect, and supervise their colleagues. And in doing so, they nurture an environment that heightens well-being and increases work performance. They increase each colleague's commitment and passion for their work.

What follows is a description of specific behaviors to amplify leadership effectiveness—the DRIVERS of engagement.

DRIVERS of Engagement

Develop
Recognize
Inform
Value
Engage
Respect
Supervise

Develop Colleagues

I coach many leaders who believe that their colleagues—their direct reports—should "just know what to do" and that they, the leader, should not have to guide them. These leaders are often hard-driving, task-oriented, and self-sufficient individuals who climbed the leadership ladder based on brute grit and an ability to independently get things done. They think others should simply do the same.

These leaders say they don't have the time to develop their colleagues. There is too much work to be done. Their direct reports need to keep up and predict what they, the leader, wants. Otherwise, the leader will re-assign the task to someone else or simply do it themselves.

The downfall of these leaders arises, predictably enough, when their high-pressure, hands-off, finger-pointing approach leaves behind a wake of disenfranchised and burned-out colleagues who feel stifled and alone. The leader's colleagues want to understand what is being asked of them, and they want to be effective, but their leader's demands are vague.

I also coach leaders who smother their colleagues with advice and mentorship. They are the "helicopter leaders" who hover over each colleague's every move. With their hyper-present coddling, they recommend each step and provide guidance through each obstacle. These leaders stifle the personal growth of colleagues. And when they move on—retiring, relocating, or leaving the organization—their colleagues are left ill-prepared without their guide. Their colleagues haven't learned to navigate the complex work environment alone.

Recall Teresa's mentor, Charlotte, who was a master at developing colleagues:

Charlotte was in charge, there was no doubt, but she had a way of empowering those she worked with and coaching them to develop their talent and skills. Teresa always felt recognized and heard—even when she was not the most "expert" or "senior" individual working on an issue. Each of her teammates functioned at the top of their game and had gone on to impressive accomplishments.

Here are leadership tactics you can use to develop colleagues:

Schedule regular one-to-one conversations. Meet one-to-one with your colleagues to identify areas in which they would like to achieve professional growth. Gain an understanding of how your colleagues see their role evolving within the organization. Discuss each colleague's progress with goals and their behaviors, and help them reflect on the obstacles they encounter. Address each colleague's experience and opportunities for development in real time, while their behaviors are top of mind and relevant, rather than as a distant and out-of-touch review of what happened months prior.

Track your interactions with colleagues. Keep track of your interactions with colleagues. Take brief notes on points of discussion and create triggers or reminders for when to next reach out. I use a tablet and a stylus to take electronic notes during conversations with colleagues. Each note resides in the electronic folder that I set up for each colleague. I can access these notes from my mobile phone, tablet, or computer. Before I meet with a colleague, I glance through my notes to catch up. This helps me remember milestones, relationships, achievements, and aspirations of colleagues.

It keeps me from repeatedly asking questions like, "Tell me again, what you were working on?" or "How many kids do you have?"

Promote group learning. Bring forward articles, books, and tutorials to share with colleagues. Nurture an environment in which colleagues learn from each other. Physicians frequently use case reviews, journal clubs, and situational simulation to learn how to best apply new information and skills. During case reviews, we discuss interesting patient care scenarios in which things went right, went wrong, or an interesting question arose. During journal clubs, we read articles and books and then discuss our perspectives. During simulations, we replicate challenging scenarios and role-play how we would respond to situations as they unfold. Many healthcare organizations create simulation centers, where they employ actors, create 3D models of the environment, and use other technologies to make the simulation experience as real as possible.

Learn to coach. Learn the differences between teaching, mentoring, coaching, supervising, and sponsoring, and how to apply each technique. You will learn about each of these "Five Hats of Effective Leaders" in Chapter Six.

NOW WHAT?

Which of the following behaviors might you incorporate to enhance engagement?

- Schedule one-to-one conversation. With whom?

- Take notes during your next one-to-one conversation.

- Create a cloud storage system for folders with names of colleagues.

- Send a brief email to a colleague to see how they are progressing on a topic previously discussed.

- Choose an article, book, or educational program for your team to review and discuss together. Which one?

Recognize Colleagues

Effective leaders recognize colleagues both for their accomplishments and for the overall value they provide to the organization. In other words, they recognize both what a person does, and who they are.[7]

Marcus Buckingham and Ashley Goodall pointed out the following in their *Harvard Business Review* article titled "The Feedback Fallacy":

Whenever you see one of your people do something that worked for you, that rocked your world just a little, stop for a minute and highlight it. By helping your team member recognize what excellence looks like for her—by saying, 'That! Yes, that!'—you're offering her the chance to gain an insight; you're highlighting a pattern that is already there within her so that she can recognize it, anchor it, re-create it, and refine it.[8]

Recognize and celebrate times when:

- Customers give praise or challenging interactions are defused.
- Work goals are achieved.
- Degrees and certificates are attained.
- Presentations go well.
- Projects are completed.
- Key values are modeled.
- Milestones are achieved—both at work and (when appropriate and with permission) in personal life.

Look beyond specific accomplishments to recognize the overall value each colleague brings to the organization. An individual's value may not be reflected in the daily metrics and milestones of work. It's easy to recognize the colleague who has the highest sales numbers, who wins the teaching award, or who bring in the most accounts, but there are also colleagues who bring tremendous value to the organization in ways that get lost in the metrics that compare each of us. Recognize overlooked and under-recognized individuals by asking yourself, "What is their plus-minus?"

Plus-Minus

Plus-Minus is a statistic used in basketball that measures an individual player's impact on the game. It measures the difference between the team's total scoring versus the opponent's total scoring when the player is in the game. Some players score the most points or have the most rebounds, but when they are in the game their team falls behind or loses their lead and the game. Those players have a low plus-minus. Conversely, there are other players who score and rebound less, but when they are in the game their team takes the lead, or adds to it and wins. Those players have a high plus-minus. The high plus-minus players enhance the overall effectiveness of their team.

Look for those individuals who bring value in ways that are not represented by your typical organizational metrics. These "no-stats all-stars" supply the spark that increases your organization's overall achievement.[9] Recognize the value they bring. And then figure out how, perhaps, you might capture their value in metrics.

Your colleagues want to be recognized for a job well done. They want to sense they are seen and that they contribute to the effectiveness of the organization. They want to know that their efforts are appreciated. Provide recognition one-to-one, in front of colleagues, and when appropriate transmit your recognition to other parts of your organization—advertise those role models of outstanding effort.

The following are leadership tactics you can apply recognize colleagues:

Send a brief note to a colleague and send a copy (cc) to their boss. In a favorite tweet, Dan Rose, a former VP of Partnerships at Facebook, praised the recognition practice of Sheryl Sandberg, COO during his time at that organization.[10]

> I frequently received emails from Sheryl with the subject "You!" It might be a note (cc Mark—the CEO of Facebook) praising me for something. More often it was a note (cc: to me) to someone on my team

(often deep in my org) praising them for something. Those little notes meant the world to their recipients.

The elegance of Sheryl's recognition behavior is multidimensional. First, it is quick. She identifies an accomplishment and sends a brief email to highlight and celebrate the colleague involved. Second, she praises her colleague in front of their leader, and when it is her own direct report, she praises them in front of her own boss—in this case the CEO (Mark). This is a form of sponsorship. Third, her recognition gives her colleague's boss an opportunity to also recognize their colleague. This gives their colleague's boss a chance to display their own leadership behaviors.

Share recognition widely. Promote accomplishments in newsletters, during meetings, on bulletin boards, as screen savers, on social media, within video or audio updates. Consider reserving the first few minutes of a meeting to recognize colleagues. It's a great way to add positive energy to discussions.

Assign recognition responsibility. Many leaders do not have time to put together recognition bulletin boards and newsletters themselves. Often, they enlist the help of others—secretaries and colleagues—to help them capture stories and achievements they can document and disseminate.

NOW WHAT?

How might you recognize your colleagues?

- Whose recent accomplishment will you highlight to your team and other leaders? How will you do so?

- Create a document with the title "Accomplishments" and write down the accomplishments of colleagues when you hear about them.

- Create a weekly (or monthly) newsletter to recognize and celebrate colleagues. Include any notes from your "Accomplishments" document.

- Create a recognition team to help you keep track of and share accomplishments of colleagues and team members.

Inform Colleagues

Ed Batista, an executive coach for Silicon Valley CEOs, notes that

> good leaders spend a material portion of their time envisioning the future—weeks, months, and even years ahead of the people around them. They peer over the horizon and get a sense of what it might be like to live there. This capability can be a tremendous asset—but only when it's coupled with the ability to influence others to adopt and act upon that same vision.[11]

Batista also advises leaders to pay attention to the Rubber Band Effect. This is what he asks you to do:

Imagine there's a rubber band connecting the leader with the people around them. When the leader travels forward in time to envision the future, the rubber band stretches. This produces a useful and necessary tension between the leader's vision and everyone else's current reality, which, under the right circumstances, can move people to adopt this vision of the future and begin to act accordingly. But if the leader runs too far ahead or pulls too hard in an effort to bring people along, the rubber band breaks. There's a rupture between the leader's vision of the future and everyone else's current reality, and the leader loses influence as a result.[12]

Leaders work at the frontier—on the edge—between the inside and the outside of their immediate work environment. They attend meetings with other leaders, they participate in senior level discussions, they work in an interdependent environment that is outside of their direct control. They note changes in strategies, workflows, competencies, and outcomes as they occur between colleagues, work units, and organizations. Effective leaders relay the news of the day, the reasoning behind organizational decision-making, and how the changing environment might affect their work. And as they inform their colleagues, they encourage discussion focused on how they and their colleagues might work together to evolve and adapt effectively to the complex environment.

Apply the following leadership tactics to inform colleagues:

Regular updates. Provide regular updates on the changes in practice and process that affect the work unit. Share what you have seen, read, and heard and reflected upon, and how you make sense of changes and challenges. You may provide updates in person, through audio and video, and through internal messaging and newsletters. Sample topics may include these:

- What are other workgroups working on?
- How are you doing with respect to resources?
- What are the key topics the CEO and board are considering?
- What are other thought leaders in your space thinking?
- What is your competition up to?
- How is technology evolving, and how might it affect your strategy?

Ask Me Anything. Be open and responsive to questions. Seek out concerns during routine meetings, during walking rounds, through anonymous survey instruments, and during special "all hands on deck" meetings. Share overheard rumors openly, ask colleagues to do the same, and then respond both transparently and nondefensively.

ROW Forward. During later chapters in this book, you will learn about a specific process you can use to bring colleagues together to create a shared sense of reality and make decisions involving complex challenges.

NOW WHAT?

How might you inform your colleagues?

- Add "Ask Me Anything" or "Rumors You've Heard" to the agenda of your next meeting to help identify and educate your colleagues about areas of concern or uncertainty.

- Which strategic challenge discussed at the senior leadership level or by thought leaders outside of the organization could you bring forward to your colleagues during a meeting, or a memo, or a retreat?

- Share the minutes (or notes) taken during a meeting with colleagues who did not attend the meeting. Share it soon after the meeting, rather than weeks later.

Embody Core Values

In his book *True North: Discover Your Authentic Leadership*, Bill George—a Harvard Business School professor and former CEO of Medtronic—advises us that a leader's effectiveness comes from a discipline of authentically embracing and embodying organizational values.[13] Authentic leaders tap into passion and perspective to bring colleagues together around a sense of shared purpose. They empower their colleagues to step up and engage.

An organization's culture is the sum of its values plus the behavior of its workforce.[14] Effective leaders bring to life the value statements displayed in the documents, placards, and screen savers that adorn the files, walls, and devices of their workplace. If an organization's core values include respect, teamwork, and innovation, the leaders display those core values in their behaviors. If core values include customer focus, agility, and continuous improvement, those values are embodied. Core values aren't just thoughts or aspirations; they are behaviors in action.

Culture = Values + Behavior

Culture is driven by action, not aspiration. Core values are best caught, not taught.[15] When a leader models values-based behavior, their actions are contagious. Their behaviors set the tone for how colleagues engage. A leader's behavior creates organizational culture.

Effective leaders embody core values not only when times are easy and the course of action is clear, but also, and perhaps more important, as they face the thorny challenges of complexity and chaos. For example, teamwork is a common core value for organizations. An effective leader in an organization that champions teamwork will invite a collaborative approach. They will seek out the unique skills and perspectives of team members. They will personify behaviors of teamwork as they engage with colleagues. And they will model teamwork even during the most pressured moments.

Ineffective leaders, on the other hand, may talk about teamwork when things are going well, but when times are tough, they fall back to lesser values. They seek the input of only a few close colleagues, ignore other perspectives, and stiflingly micromanage team members. And as they display behaviors that are the opposite of the core values they espouse, they appear disingenuous, untrustworthy, and perhaps deceitful. The value slogans that line the walls of their organization start to feel empty.

Gaps arise when leaders disregard the deliberate practice of transforming statements of core values into behaviors in action. In a study that appeared in the *MIT Sloan Management Review*, researchers found that more than 80 percent of nearly seven hundred companies published an official set of corporate values on their website.[16] Integrity, collaboration, customer focus, and respect were, for example, the four most used terms to represent corporate values. The researchers asked whether the organizations and their leadership displayed the behaviors invoked in their values—did they walk the talk? Unfortunately, the data showed little correlation between the memorialized values and the behaviors within corporate culture.

Consider the following list of corporate values:

- Respect: We treat others as we would like to be treated ourselves.
- Integrity: We work with customers and prospects openly, honestly, and sincerely.
- Communication: We have an obligation to communicate. Here, we take the time to talk with one another . . . and to listen.
- Excellence: We are satisfied with nothing less than the very best in everything we do.

Unfortunately, these are the value statements for Enron, once a thriving energy company, now an infamous example of willful corporate corruption.[17] The CEO of Enron was convicted of eighteen counts of fraud and conspiracy after their company filed for what at the time was the largest bankruptcy in American history.[18] While the values of respect and integrity were written in the words of corporate documents, they were absent both in the behaviors of Enron's senior leaders and in the actions of the conforming and colluding colleagues they led.

It's not the list of core values that is important. It is the embodiment of the behaviors that the core values represent. Those organizations that hold steady to their core values have an advantage. Core values serve as a sort of behavioral playbook for how individuals are to engage with each other and with customers. Without a behavioral playbook, there is a loss of synchrony, and execution becomes muddled.

Let's be clear. Values alone do not make a company successful. Success comes from a combination of skills, knowledge, hard work, market focus, and many other factors. But if you and your colleagues are not engaged together with shared values, you compete against yourselves, in addition to the market.

NOW WHAT?

How do you demonstrate core values in action?

- Memorize the core values of your organization and consider the ways in which your behaviors reflect or demonstrate the opposite of each core value.

- Interview colleagues to capture stories that highlight core values in action.

- Discuss an organizational core value and the associated behaviors with colleagues during your next meeting.

- Consider how a proposed solution to a challenge reflects the mission and values of your organization.

- Consider whether the core values of your organization need to be refreshed or updated.

Engage Colleagues

Many leaders overly rely on the formal organizational structure as they make decisions. These leaders convene meetings of individuals with formal organizational titles, they consider the challenge, and they decide. They use a top-down approach that fails to engage other colleagues in important decisions. There are certainly many times when this works—times when this is the most effective way to make decisions and get things done. But at other times, and if the practice isn't deliberately considered and held in check, such a process risks alienating colleagues, depressing employee morale, and promoting suboptimal decision-making.

Egosystem versus Ecosystem

Consider a typical formal organizational chart. At the top there is the CEO, and then the vice presidents, and then directors and managers. While titles may vary within different organizations, the level of decision-making power is clear. The CEO has more power to make decisions, to hire and fire, and to set strategy than do the vice presidents, who in turn have more power than directors, and so on.

An overreliance on titles and formal leadership roles promotes what author and artist Austin Kleon calls an organizational *egosystem*—a decision-making structure tailored to the egos and blind spots of the few; the (en)titled.[19, 20] We learned in previous chapters that decisions based on individual expertise, rather than on shared perspectives of complex reality, decrease the likelihood of success. On the other hand, the likelihood of success is increased when we engage colleagues to share perspectives. Effective decision-making, especially in complex settings, occurs within a collaborative and engaged organizational *ecosystem*.

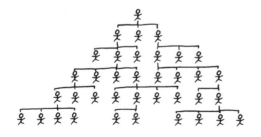 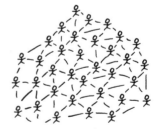

Egosystem   **Ecosystem**

It isn't practical—nor would I suggest—that a leader survey every colleague before they make each challenging decision. However, leaders need to be alert to recognize potential benchmark decisions. Benchmark decisions involve complex challenges that significantly affect the well-being of colleagues. These decisions provide leaders an opportunity to engage colleagues to bolster values, increase well-being, and improve outcomes. On the contrary, when benchmark decisions are decided within the egosystem of formal leadership—without the engagement of colleagues—the leader risks the creation of discord. When leaders deliberately recognize opportunities to engage the ecosystem of colleagues, they not only increase the effectiveness of these decisions, but they also enhance their colleagues' sense of autonomy and competence within their environment, and engender supportive relationships.[21]

Teresa, the chief medical officer, read about a large physician group in the Twin Cities of Minnesota that successfully implemented a new EHR system. She recalled that the leaders of that physician group recognized the limitations of the egosystem of their formal organizational hierarchy, and wisely decided that cascading top-down decision-making during such a complex implementation process might not yield the best results. The group enlisted the help of Keyhubs, Inc., a Minneapolis-based software and services firm specializing in organizational social network analysis, to understand the informal network—the ecosystem—of influence within the hierarchy of the clinic.[22]

Keyhubs researchers posed a series of confidential questions to the clinic staff to understand the collaborative ecosystem. For example, they asked:

- Who is a critical knowledge leader—the "go-to person"—
  in how to get operational tasks completed effectively in the
  clinic?
- Who do you think is most open to and positive in their support of change?
- Which people cling to the comfort of the old ways of doing
  things and are most likely to slow down or block the forward
  momentum of change?

In each case they asked the respondent to name three of their colleagues in their answer. From the responses, Keyhubs created a map—not the neat blocks of the organizational hierarchy—but the slightly more disjointed circles of an informal ecosystem.

Formal influence

Informal influence

And as they examined the results, they noted some surprising aspects. They found that the individual, for example, who would be most looked up to as a leader during times of change could be an individual who held no formal leadership title, whereas the individual most likely to block innovation might be the formal leader. The hidden informal network is strong, and it is crucial to leverage the perspectives of this ecosystem to overcome the biases enmeshed within the expertise of formal leaders. Within the ecosystem of your organization, there are "leaders without titles" who are crucial to organizational success. Identify these individuals, give them resources and decision-making power, and help them develop.

Scenius

In his book *Creating Better Futures*, James Ogilvy, the founding and managing director of the Global Business Network, noted that "all of us are smarter than any of us. Different members of a team bring different resources to a team. We know different things. We have different strengths. We can make up for one another's weaknesses."[23]

Our most effective leaders ascribe to the "leaders at all levels" framework when facing complex challenges.[24] They engage colleagues to work together to solve the most difficult challenges. These leaders bring together the collective genius of individuals to generate a group wisdom known as "scenius" [pronounced: seen-yus].

According to Brian Eno, the multiplatinum-selling producer, composer, and artist who coined the term "scenius," genius is individual, whereas scenius leverages "the intelligence and the intuition of a whole scene. It is the communal form of the concept of the genius."[25, 26] Eno has experienced the power of scenius while producing albums by such bands as Coldplay and U2. Each band has a charismatic singer with a distinct point of view, but the scenius of band members, producers, and engineers produces the best work.

The power of scenius has inspired many groups of collective genius.[27] The Inklings, a group of authors in 1930s England, would meet on Thursdays to read and discuss their unfinished works.[28] Warren Lewis, a founding Inkling, spoke of the value of alternate perspectives as he noted, "We were no mutual admiration society: praise for good work was unstinted, but censure for bad work—or even not-so-good work—was often brutally frank."[29] J.R.R. Tolkien and C.S Lewis, two members of the Inklings, would eventually sell three of the top five best-selling fantasy books of all time.[30]

Another demonstration of scenius lay within the plywood offices of Building 20 at the Massachusetts Institute of Technology. This ramshackle structure housed researchers from twenty different academic disciplines—including linguists, mathematicians, engineers, physicists, neurophysiologists, and computer scientists.[31] Within its walls, individuals from multiple disciplines would meet and collaborate to produce the first atomic clock, the first radar, the modern school of linguistics, and the first programmable transistor-based computer.

Kevin Kelly, the founding editor of *Wired* magazine, described key elements that promote scenius:[32]

- There is a mutual appreciation of the value each individual brings to the organization. Differences in opinion are prized and the unorthodox or independent-minded are protected rather than rejected.
- There is a rapid exchange of ideas and tools and techniques. As new insights and approaches are discovered they are freely shared rather than guarded. Individuals within a scenius look at each other's work, they contribute ideas, and they incorporate the genius of others into their own work.[33]
- Success is claimed and celebrated by the entire scene. There are individual achievements, but individual success is catalyzed by the networked genius of the organization.

Leaders who deliberately build the ecosystem and develop the scenius within their organization promote a more engaging and effective workplace.

NOW WHAT?

How could you better engage your colleagues in decision-making?

How are you limiting the engagement of your colleagues?

How do you identify and leverage both the genius and scenius of your colleagues?

Consider applying the following suggestions:

- Use the ROW Forward framework discussed later in this book to engage colleagues at all levels of the organization in the decision-making and implementation related to an important, complex challenge.

- Recognize and engage the "leaders without a title" at all levels of the organization to serve on committees, participate in key discussions, and help design key processes.

- Provide startup funding and/or the support of resources for the initial development of projects at all levels of the organization.

- Provide leadership training and further development opportunities for these "leaders without a title."

Respect Colleagues

Effective leaders treat each colleague with respect and dignity. They pay attention to each colleague's psychological well-being, and in doing so they promote engagement. They support each colleague's sense of purpose, their need for autonomy, and the importance of their personal and professional growth. They appreciate diversity of perspective, culture, gender, race, background, and experience. They regard the development of a diverse team of individuals as being an essential component to effective decision-making in complex environments.

Throughout this book I prefer to refer to individuals as colleagues, rather than as direct reports, or employees, or subordinates. My sense is that our most effective leaders respect each of the individuals with whom they work and view them as colleagues. Colleagues may be of different ages. They may have more or less experience and status. They may be a direct report, be on a similar level, or be at a higher level in the formal organizational structure. Effective leaders regard individuals as colleagues, each deserving of similar levels of mutual respect.

NOW WHAT?

How might you increase the diversity—and the decision-making effectiveness—of your organization?

How might you develop your workforce and your leadership team to reflect the complexity of the domains you serve?

Supervise Colleagues

Supervision involves both stepping in to serve the needs of each colleague and stepping back to serve the needs of the organization.

When you step in, you focus on the well-being and effectiveness of each individual. You ensure that each colleague has the resources needed to perform their work, you safeguard the environment to encourage positive interpersonal relations, you champion alignment of each individual's sense of purpose with organizational mission and values, you promote autonomy and personal growth, and you maintain an environment where it is safe to admit and learn from mistakes.

When you step back, you focus on the well-being and effectiveness of the organization as a whole. You steward resources, you monitor performance and expectations, you ensure alignment with legal and regulatory constructs, you facilitate effective decision-making, and you hold yourself accountable for the successful implementation of organizational strategy.

If you choose to optimize the well-being of an individual at the expense of the organization, you risk undermining organizational strategy and impairing the effectiveness of colleagues. On the other hand, if you choose to optimize the effectiveness of the organization at the expense of an individual's well-being, you risk the development of burnout with all of its negative consequences. Supervision is not easy. During times of complexity, you and your colleagues face difficult circumstances. When necessary, you may need to make difficult decisions that negatively impact some individuals, in order to improve the effectiveness of the organization, but you do so with a knowledge of the relationship between individual and organizational well-being.

Supervise Yourself

Effective supervision includes an ongoing examination of your own behaviors. Ask your colleagues to rate your leadership behaviors. You could ask them directly how you are doing, but this tactic may result in empty feedback that leaves out important uncomfortable details.

An alternative approach to discovering how your colleagues perceive your leadership behaviors involves the use of either an organizational engagement and culture survey or a short questionnaire—such as the leadership behavior survey discussed at

the beginning of this chapter.[34] You might, for example, distribute a short leadership behavior survey around the time you perform annual reviews. The result of the survey will provide specific and actionable detail about how your behaviors are perceived—and you can work to improve any lagging behaviors.

Revisiting Teresa

Having developed an understanding of the DRIVERS of engagement, Teresa focused on the specific leadership behaviors that would enhance engagement. As Teresa's cross-functional team worked to implement the new EHR, she intermittently sent colleagues a brief leadership behavior survey. This helped her identify specific behaviors she could focus on to improve her effectiveness. She maintained a list to keep track of each colleague's activities and made sure to focus on the DRIVERS of engagement.

One of the leadership behavior surveys revealed something unexpected to Teresa. Her colleagues sensed that their efforts within the EHR workgroup were going unrecognized outside of the workgroup. Many of Teresa's colleagues on the EHR project team did not report directly to her; rather, they reported to other leaders within the organization. And those leaders had no idea about what their mutual colleague on the EHR team was doing. In response, Teresa started to send brief emails to highlight the accomplishments of each colleague—with a cc: to each colleague's boss. For example, one individual on her team was a surgical nursing leader. Teresa's email to that nurse also copied the Chief Nursing Officer to recognize their mutual colleague's "outstanding contribution."

Although planning the launch of the EHR was quite challenging as the team maneuvered around several unexpected barriers, the implementation was successful, and the team remained both highly effective and engaged throughout the process.

What's Next?

In Chapter Six, you will discover specific tactics you may use to improve the effectiveness of your one-to-one conversations with colleagues. You will be introduced to the Five Hats of Effective Leaders and will learn how and when to wear the different hats of teacher, mentor, coach, supervisor, and sponsor as you meet with individual colleagues.

Executive Summary

> ➤ Research highlights eight specific leadership behaviors that directly affect levels of burnout and engagement of a leader's direct reports. Engagement increases and burnout decreases when a leader:

   1. Holds career development conversations with each colleague.

   2. Empowers each colleague to do their job.

   3. Treats each colleague with dignity and respect.

4. Provides helpful feedback and coaching on each colleague's performance.

5. Recognizes each colleague for a job well done.

6. Keeps each colleague informed about changes taking place within their company or organization.

7. Encourages each colleague to develop their talent and skills.

8. Encourages each colleague to suggest ideas for improvement.

➤ Effective leaders develop, recognize, inform, value, engage, respect, and supervise colleagues. These are the DRIVERS of engagement.

➤ Effective leaders schedule regular one-to-one conversations with colleagues, track and remember the information discussed, reach out directly through email and brief conversations, adjust the frequency of their engagement to each colleague's needs, and promote group learning.

➤ Effective leaders recognize colleagues for their accomplishments and for the overall value they provide to the organization. In other words, they recognize both what a person does, and who they are.[35] They use a plus-minus approach to identify the value that colleagues bring in ways that may not be represented in organizational metrics. They keep each colleague's leader apprised of significant accomplishments, share recognition widely with other colleagues, and create a process to capture recognition opportunities.

➤ Leaders work at the frontier—on the edge—between the inside and the outside of their immediate work environment.

Effective leaders keep colleagues informed through regular report-outs using multiple mechanisms and media as well as through ask-me-anything sessions and by directly involving colleagues in complex decision-making.

➤ An organization's culture is the sum of its values plus the behavior of its workforce.[36] Core values are best caught, not taught.[37] When a leader models values-based behavior, their actions are contagious. Their behaviors set the tone for how colleagues engage. Their behaviors create organizational culture.

➤ Effective leaders recognize the limitations of the individual genius within the egosystem of formal organizational leadership structures when facing complex challenges. These leaders ascribe to a "leaders at all levels" framework as they tap into the collective wisdom—the scenius—within the collaborative informal ecosystem of engaged colleagues.

➤ Effective leaders treat each colleague with respect and dignity. They pay attention to each colleague's psychological well-being, and by doing so they promote engagement. They support each colleague's sense of purpose, their need for autonomy, and the importance of their personal and professional growth. They appreciate diversity of perspective, culture, gender, race, background, and experience. They see a diverse team of individuals as an essential component of effective decisions in complex environments.

➤ Supervision is a balancing act involving both stepping in to serve the needs of each colleague and stepping back to serve the needs of the organization. When you step in, you focus on the well-being and effectiveness of each individual. When you step back, you focus on the well-being and effectiveness of the organization. Too much of either risks undermining the other.

6

LEAD DURING ONE-TO-ONE CONVERSATIONS

Jules is the CEO of a rapidly growing software company he cofounded with two close friends. They recently completed a successful series A funding round, and they're focused on quickly increasing their customer base and scaling to meet demand.

So they're on a hiring spree—which has changed how they operate. Previously they personally directed organizational workflow from their shared loft. Now they rely on a distributed network of remote teams of individuals who live all over the world.

Jules is beginning to feel both out of touch and overwhelmed. Earlier this morning, he participated in two video chats that left him doubting his leadership skills. One conversation was with a colleague seeking advice about a project Jules previously led. The other conversation was with a colleague who was feeling burned out. Jules was direct with each colleague. He told each of them what needed to be done and how to move forward, but in both cases, his advice seemed to fall flat.

Jules wonders how to become a more effective CEO. He realizes that he needs to develop different skills. He feels comfortable setting organizational goals and strategy, but he feels lost when dealing with the individual needs and concerns of colleagues. He has a nagging sense that a seasoned leader would navigate similar challenges more effectively.

In previous chapters, we discussed how expertise is useful in some situations and limiting in others. Jules is experiencing this firsthand. He is rarely stumped, and he instantly knows what to do in most cases. Unfortunately, his well-honed sense of expertise and a habit of getting things done impair his ability to inspire and lead others. To lead more effectively, Jules needs to adopt less of a "this is what I think" approach and develop more of a "what do you think" approach. He needs to learn when to put aside his expertise. He needs to adopt more nuanced conversational tactics.

In this chapter, you will learn about the Five Hats of Effective Leaders. You will recognize how you might "wear" each hat and switch hats during one-to-one conversations with colleagues. When you adopt the five hats approach, you step up from your expertise and enhance your ability to listen, understand, and develop colleagues. You help your colleagues find their own answers. And in doing so, you amplify the collective wisdom of your organization.

The Five Hats of Effective Leaders

Effective leaders wear the hats of teacher, mentor, coach, supervisor, and sponsor.[1] Each hat represents a distinct tactic or approach that a leader may use in one-to-one conversations with colleagues. The goal in all of these is to help the colleague develop the skills, behaviors, and reasoning for success in the complex world.

To paraphrase influential management consultant Peter Drucker, leadership lifts a person's vision to higher sights, raises a person's performance to a higher standard, and builds a personality beyond its normal limitations.[2] One-to-one developmental conversations with colleagues will help you achieve these leadership aspirations.

A wonderful aspect of the Five Hats approach is that it takes the pressure off of you, the leader. You don't need to know what to do, you don't need to have a response, you don't need to shoulder the burden in every moment. There are many times when your greatest value comes from your ability to help colleagues think through their challenges in their own way. As you shift your leadership from one of knowing and deciding to one of coaching and facilitating, your effectiveness increases.

Lauren, a physician scientist I coached, said she lacked what it took to be a leader. "I'm an introvert. I don't like being in the spotlight. I just want to advance the science. I don't have what it takes to order people around."

She was an internationally respected oncologist with a research laboratory supported by two prestigious grants. She had a schedule filled with colleagues seeking her mentorship. And she had been nominated by her department chair as an up-and-coming leader within the organization. As part of her leadership development, she would meet monthly with me as her coach each month.

"I just don't have the ability to lead on a large scale. Sure, I can run a research lab, but that doesn't mean I can lead at scale. I'm not one of those people who can simply walk into a room and make a decision for someone. I can't just show up to a meeting and feel comfortable throwing out some opinion."

Over the next several months of coaching, we discussed how she dealt with tension between the postdoctorate scientists in her lab as well as her approach to meetings with senior organizational leaders, and she identified tasks she might delegate to others.

As we progressed through her daily challenges, I interwove concepts of coaching and teaching as a leader. And we role-played scenarios in which she would wear "different hats" during difficult conversations.

She began to realize that while she may not know all of the answers, her drive to find answers and to understand—the traits that had fueled her success as a physician scientist—were, in fact, traits of effective leadership. In most scenarios, she did not need to know the answer; she just needed to figure out how to get to an answer.

She was a natural teacher, coach, and sponsor. And her effectiveness as a leader soon played out as she accepted a role overseeing a crucial organizational restructuring.

What follows is a summary of each of the five leadership hats and an overview of how you might wear each of them during a one-to-one conversation. You will learn the benefits and limitations of each approach. And finally, you will discover how to switch hats during a conversation to optimize leadership effectiveness.

The Five Hats of Effective Leaders

Teach
Teach to help your colleague learn new knowledge and skills

Mentor
Mentor to help your colleague consider the world through *your experienced eyes.*

Coach
Coach to help your colleague investigate and consider their perspectives of the world through their *own* eyes.

Supervise
Supervise to oversee and promote the day-to-day and long-term effectiveness of your colleague.

Sponsor
Sponsor to use your influence and connections to provide opportunities for your colleague

Teach

When you teach, you convey new information and skills. You reveal knowledge previously unknown. And as you impart knowledge, you open new ways for your colleague to interpret their experiences.

But before you jump in to teach, it's best to figure out what your colleague knows. You can do this by asking simple questions:

- "What is your understanding of our marketing approach?"
- "What do you know about how the vesting schedule is structured?"
- "What is your comfort level with performing this skill?"

Then, if you sense an opportunity to teach, you ask your colleague:

- "Would it be helpful if I told you what I know about . . .?"
- "Would you like me to show you the recommended steps?"

If, on the other hand, in a fit of expertise, you skip those questions and jump forward to teach without first understanding your colleague's level of knowledge and gauging their interest in your teachings, you risk wasting time. You might talk over their head, or even worse, disrespect them by telling them things they already know. You risk being interpreted as condescending or patronizing.

When you employ an opening line of questions, you not only reveal teaching opportunities but also increase the specificity and the effectiveness of your teachings. Your colleague's answers provide information that allows you to focus on the specific aspects of the marketing approach that are confusing to them. You can elaborate on specific parts of the skills that need further explanation. Additionally, as you learn about your colleague's knowledge gaps, you reveal what may be similar knowledge gaps among other colleagues in a similar position. Perhaps you need to address your overall approach to how you inform and bring colleagues on board.

Knowledge and skill-building are good, but teaching has limitations. Your colleague may have knowledge and skills but no idea how to apply them to their real-world issues. They may be fearful about applying their knowledge or skill. They may not understand how their learning applies in an evolving environment. They may not know what to do when they encounter disagreement or an alternative approach. During such instances, you have an opportunity to switch from wearing the hat of teacher to donning one of the other hats—such as coach or mentor—to help your colleague move forward.

NOW WHAT?

Think of a time when you taught your colleague without first knowing what they understood about the topic. You did not ask permission to teach. You overplayed your expertise.

How did that go? How might you have approached the conversation differently?

Mentor

When you mentor, you help your colleague envision the world through your own experienced eyes. As your colleague relays their experiences, you have an instinct of what might occur, what you would do, and how they might move forward.

Mentoring is like teaching in that you transfer information to your colleague, but what you impart comes from knowledge and wisdom rooted in your own experience.[3] You have "been there and done that," and your background and expertise reveal alternative options and strategies for your colleague to consider.

The following statements provide a cue that you are wearing the mentor hat:

- Given my experience, this is what you might consider . . ."
- "If I were you, I would . . ."
- "The way I see it, you have two options . . ."

When mentoring, you not only convey your experienced perspectives, but you also relay how you have seen other colleagues approach similar situations:

- "I had another colleague in a similar situation. Here is what they did . . ."
- "In my experience, I have approached the situation by . . . , but I had another colleague approach it in this way . . ."

Similar to teaching, it's a good practice to first ask your colleague if your mentorship would be helpful:

- "Would it be helpful if I shared my perspective?"
- "Would it be helpful if I shared what I have seen work in similar circumstances?"
- "Would it help if I shared my experience?"

While your experiences and perspectives can be helpful, mentoring has limitations. First, your colleague may not want your views. While you and I agree that your viewpoints are impeccable, and everyone would benefit from your perspective, some of your colleagues may not agree. They may want to develop their own views.

Second, your perspectives may contain blind spots. You may inadvertently miss key factors or viewpoints. Or your views may differ dramatically from others' views. And if your mentoring carries significant weight, you may pass along your blind spots and errant perspectives.

Another limitation of mentoring occurs when your colleague "just wants *you* to give *them* the *answer.*" Your colleague may want to offload their decision-making to you. And while it might feel good to direct your colleague based upon your seasoned expertise, you risk stifling their ability to construct their own solution. Your solution might help your colleague solve their problem now, but may fail to leverage what is best for them when considering their own future goals and potential. While your colleague may seek *your answers*, their personal and professional growth relies on them developing their own ability to reconcile conflicting perspectives.[4] They need to learn to make sense of the world on their own.

The mentor hat is comfortable, woven from our own experience and expertise. But now take it off and put on a different leadership hat to help your colleague step back into their own perspective and challenge others.

NOW WHAT?

Think of a colleague who seeks your answers too often.

How might you help them develop the ability to find their own answers?

Coach

When you coach, you help your colleague make sense of the world based on their own experiences, perspectives, and beliefs—through their own eyes. While wearing the coaching hat, you put aside your subject-matter expertise, and you view *your colleague as the expert* of their own experience.

While coaching, you ask open-ended questions to promote reflection and reframing:

- "What would you like to do moving forward?"
- "How would you approach this challenge?"
- "Given that, what are your thoughts?"
- "What is your worry about using that approach?"
- "What else might you do?"

As you coach, you listen to how your colleague answers your questions, note their reactions, and keep track of their various responses. Their responses inform both you and how you communicate with your colleague.

Just as adding memory empowers a computer to work more efficiently, as a coach, you "add RAM" to your colleague's cognitive process. You enable more powerful sense-making. You help your colleague process complex challenges and move to action.

THE *GROW* MODEL

The GROW model described by former race-car driver Sir John Whitmore in his book, *Coaching for Performance: The Principles and Practice of Coaching and Leadership*, is a simple but powerful coaching framework.[5] GROW is a mnemonic that identifies a sequence of themes for questions—Goal, Reality, Options, Will—that you may follow during a coaching conversation with a colleague.

Here are examples of questions you could ask a colleague during the different phases of a coaching conversation using the GROW model.

G Goal
What do you want?

R Reality
What is happening?

O Options
What could do this?

W Will
What will you do?

Goal. You help your colleague look toward the future and express their desired outcome.

- "What's on your mind?"
- "What would you like to talk about?"
- "What would you like to accomplish?"

Reality. You help your colleague consider the current reality of their situation.

- "What is the situation?"
- "What are your thoughts?"
- "What is important about this for you?"
- "What do you think might happen?"
- "Who else is affected?"
- "What would happen if you did nothing?"
- "How much control do you have in this situation?"
- "What do you think you might be missing?"

Options. You help your colleague brainstorm multiple ways to achieve their goal.

- "What would you like to do?"
- "What if you couldn't do that? What else might you do?"
- "What if _____happened?"

Will. You help your colleague choose the specific actions they will take to achieve their goal.

- "How are you going to move forward?"
- "What specifically will you do?"
- "When are you going to do it?"
- "What might get in your way?"
- "Who do you need to involve?"
- "How will you know you have succeeded?"

Let's revisit Jules, the CEO of the rapidly growing software company. Recall that he had a conversation with a colleague who was trying to figure out how to best move forward on a project. However, when Jules offered his advice, his recommendations fell flat.

Having read about the GROW model, Jules had an opportunity to meet with another colleague the following day to discuss a similarly challenging issue. This time he decided to use a different approach. He put on the leadership hat of a coach.

Goal:

Jules: "Hi Watts![6] What's on your mind?"

Watts: "I'm trying to figure out how to improve the productivity of our team."

Reality:

Jules: "What's the situation?"

Watts: "We have a big range of productivity across the different members of our team. Some of my teammates are very productive, while others, not so much. And I'm thinking about making all of our productivity data transparent."

Jules: "What are your thoughts?"

Watts: "I think we need to liberate productivity data. When we hide the data, people make up their own stories, and then I have to try to manage all of the different stories and expectations."

Jules: "Interesting. What do you think might happen if you made the data transparent?"

Watts: "I think many people would like it. But I worry that some of our colleagues would feel exposed, like I had betrayed their trust. And this would add to the stress we already feel as we move to launch the new product. It might divide the team."

Jules: "What if you did nothing?"

Watts: "Well, we need to accelerate our productivity, or we will not meet our deadline. We need to do something."

Options:

Jules: "What would you like to do?"

Watts: "I'd like just to release the data transparently. And then I can manage those individuals who feel exposed."

Jules: "That sounds like a good idea. But let's imagine—for the sake of discussion—you couldn't do that. What else might you do?"

Watts: "Well, I suppose I could release the productivity data and only show each individual their own name. They could see how they compare to everyone else, but the other names would be confidential."

Will:

Jules: "Interesting idea. How are you going to move forward?"

Watts: "I think I will initially release the data in a way that allows individuals to see how they are doing but keeps their identity anonymous to others. This will give each person time to improve without feeling like others are judging them. And then, in a few weeks, I will release all of the productivity data transparently."

Jules: "Excellent. Be sure to tell me if there is anything I can do to help you."

Watts: "Thanks, Jules!"

As you can see, the coaching approach is quite different from a mentoring process. When you coach, you take advantage of what your colleague knows. You help them develop their perspectives. And you keep your opinions to yourself.

NOW WHAT?

Think of a conversation with a colleague that you have scheduled during the next few weeks. Perhaps they are struggling with a decision.

How might you employ the GROW model of coaching? What questions might you ask your colleague in order to clarify their goal, reality, options, and will?

Click a Phrase

When you click on a link within a news story on your mobile device, you reveal more information and background. This data adds to the storyline. Similarly, while coaching colleagues, as you listen closely, you begin to hear phrases you might want to investigate—might want to click on. Words that, if investigated, would provide further insight into the storyline of your colleague's thinking, emotions, and behaviors.

Each of us has specific phrases we use to speed up the flow of our thoughts and conversations. These words serve as shorthand, an abbreviated code, of our deeper thoughts and perspectives. Interestingly and confusingly, the same words may mean completely different things to different people. Think of what common terms like "fair" or "success" or "manage" might mean to your colleagues and yourself. The exact same words may encode distinct and divergent ranges of information, opinions, and emotions. Therefore, as a leader, it makes sense to click on—to investigate—words and phrases to discover meaning and promote a more nuanced understanding of what is being discussed.

For example, recall that Jules' colleague said, "I can manage those individuals." But what did Watts mean when they said: "manage"? Would they meet privately with each individual to discuss opportunities for improvement? Would they appoint someone else to oversee the objective? Would they fire people? Jules could have clicked on the phrase in reply to Watts by inquiring, "How would you manage those individuals?

Your colleague says:

You wonder what your colleague means when they use the word "manage":

So, you *click on* the word "manage":

And your colleague explains:

I will meet each of my low-performing colleagues on Monday to show them their date. I will **clarify** my expectations for the future. And I will offer both my **support** and **encouragement**.

Sometimes our shorthand phrases conceal blind spots, fears, and incorrect assumptions. Our words disguise generalizations, distorted thoughts, and critical variables that we tune out or omit.[7] When you explore phrasing, you reveal the embedded meanings, emotions, and perspectives, and you provide your colleague an opportunity to challenge limiting assumptions and show further options.

As you read through each of the following statements, think of the phrase (or phrases) you might click on while coaching a colleague:

- "This will not work."
- "Everybody knows it is true."
- "The sales team is difficult to work with."

Now, let's consider each of these phrases individually.

"*This* will not work."

Clickable phrase: "This."
Coaching thoughts: What is meant by the word "this"? This step?

This project? This approach? This relationship? The critical information has been deleted—and replaced by the word "this."

Coaching question: "Interesting. Please tell me more. What specifically will never work?"

"Everybody knows *it* is true."

Clickable phrase: "Everybody."

Coaching thoughts: When an individual uses terms like everybody and nobody, I want to investigate those phrases. It seems like a perspective that may be distorted—like gazing at a warped house of mirrors that reveals multiple reflections of our own view. We might, for example, find through further conversation that some colleagues—not all—think *it* is false, not true. Clarify the specific individuals that the word "everybody" references, and you more accurately discover the magnitude of the situation.

Coaching question: "When you say 'everybody,' who specifically are you referring to?"

Clickable phrase: "It."

Coaching thoughts: This seems like another deletion of crucial information. What is meant by the word "it"?

Coaching question: "You had mentioned that everybody knows *it* is true. Help me understand—everybody knows *what* is true?"

"That *the sales team* is *difficult to work with.*"

Clickable phrase: "The sales team."

Coaching thoughts: This is a generalization that treats every individual on the sales team as if they are all just one person. My guess is that some individuals are difficult to work with, while others make the job easy.

Coaching question: "Help me understand. Who specifically on the sales team is difficult to work with?"

Clickable phrase: "Difficult to work with."

Coaching thoughts: I'd like to know more details about the difficult working situation. Difficult to work with because they disagree with your approach? Difficult to work with because they do not deliver results? Difficult to work with because they are a covert team of extraverted robots sent from outer space to destroy our company?

Coaching question: "In what way is the sales team difficult to work with?"

NOW WHAT?

What are common phrases you hear in your work environment? Think of how these phrases may hide generalizations, distortions, and deletions of information.

How might you click on some of these phrases during one-to-one conversations to increase understanding and awareness?

Be aware. Coaching also has limitations.

Coaching is a learned skill. The more you study and deliberately practice the various coaching approaches, the better you will become. There is a big difference in the skills between those who read a chapter on coaching and practice it, those who attend a several-day course, and those who study coaching in graduate school. Coaching is a discipline with many facets and levels. Be prepared. You may feel a bit awkward as you initially try on the coaching hat. Keep at it.

While coaching can help expand your colleague's perspectives, your colleague may have knowledge gaps, fail to see possibilities, or not understand the ramification of their actions. In such cases, your open-ended questions may lead to dead-end answers. And your discussions may yield little progress. In these cases, take off the coaching hat and use a different approach. For example, you might sense that your colleague has a knowledge gap. Move from coaching to teaching. You might think an experienced perspective would help. Put on the mentor hat. Later on, during the conversation, you can return to coaching to help your colleague contemplate the new information.

Coaching conversations are not meant to catch your colleague off-guard. Approach your colleague positively, with sincere interest and well-meaning intentions. If you sense that a colleague feels uneasy, embarrassed, or defensive, you may need to back off. You may need to reiterate your respect. You may need to empathize and provide further support for your colleague's feelings and concerns. Or it might be a good time to switch hats.

Supervise

Effective leaders are supervisors.

When you wear the hat of the supervisor, you:

- Set, nurture, and protect mission, values, and strategy.
- Oversee the implementation and accomplishment of tasks, projects, and roles.
- Delegate tasks and set deadlines.
- Steward the resources needed to accomplish strategic goals.
- Identify and champion the metrics of high performance.
- Maintain an effective and responsive management structure.
- Recruit and hire qualified colleagues.
- Recognize and reward high performers.
- Improve or remove underperformers.
- Resolve conflict.

When you supervise, you oversee your colleagues, your team, and your organization's day-to-day and long-term effectiveness. You identify and direct the removal of obstacles. You ensure that strategic goals are accomplished. You champion mission and values. You configure your team to work at its best.

However, you can overplay the role of supervisor. And when you do, you may become overly prescriptive. You lead through edict. You favor a "boss-to-direct report" rather than a "colleague-to-colleague" style of conversation. You adopt what I call the GRR! Model of Leadership.

GRR! is a mnemonic that describes a process by which you overly impose your supervision on colleagues.

- **G**oal: You tell your colleague the goal.
- **R**eality: You tell them how you make sense of the situation.
- **R**un along!: You tell them what to do.

There are times when a GRR! approach is needed. For example, in Chapter Two, we discussed chaos. During chaos, a leader does not have the time to wear several hats. They need to make decisions and move to action.

But outside of chaos, the GRR! approach stifles conversation. It impedes the development of shared perspectives and shared adaptation. It fails to lift the vision, raise the performance, and build the personality of colleagues. It impairs your ability to lead effectively. Peter Drucker would disapprove.

Use supervision during one-to-one conversation sparingly and with focused intent. Consider two examples of supervisory dialogue and consider how a change from the supervisor hat would enhance the discussion and prevent GRR! moments.

In the first example, a colleague has performed exceptionally.

> You: "I just wanted to tell you that your performance has been outstanding. You are our top salesperson. Our customers rave about your level of knowledge and support."
>
> Colleague: "Thank you!"

You could simply end the conversation there—a very nice interaction.

On the other hand, you could put on another leadership hat. For example, you could decide to ask a series of coaching questions:

- "What behaviors have been key to your achieving such a high level of performance?"
- "What things might we change to make your job even easier?"
- "How do you think we might improve our overall effectiveness even more?"

The coaching questions in this circumstance enhance the effectiveness of your positive feedback. And it offers both you and your colleague an opportunity to learn and improve.

In a second example, a colleague is underperforming.

> You: "I wanted to make you aware that your sales performance is below expectations. You currently rank in the bottom 25 percent of sales overall. Additionally, your sales per client have been decreasing compared to that of your colleagues."

A less effective approach would be to continue using the GRR! Model.

> You: "We need you to improve your sales per client and increase your number of sales leads. And we need to see a significant improvement by next quarter."
>
> Colleague: "Okay. Yes, I agree. Thank you."

A more effective approach would involve the changing of leadership hats.

You might ask coaching questions:

- "What challenges are you facing?"
- "What approach seems most effective?"
- "What is your sense of what we see in these metrics?"
- "How do you think you might improve your sales per client?"
- "Who might you reach out to for additional helpful feedback?"

You might mentor:

- "Based on what I am seeing, I suggest you . . ."
- "This is what I have seen others do that has worked in a similar situation . . ."

You might teach:

- "Would it be helpful if I taught you a more effective way to use our customer relationship management software?"
- "Would you like me to teach you more effective scripting? It could help you increase your sales per client."

Each of the hats enhances your approach. You might wear each of the leadership hats several times during a conversation to increase the impact of your supervisory statements.

NOW WHAT?

Think about a conversation you need to have with an underperforming colleague.

How might you enhance your supervision by also wearing the hats of teacher and coach?

Sponsor

The final leadership hat is sponsor. When you sponsor a colleague, you use your influence and connections to promote your colleague. You highlight your colleague's skills and capabilities with other colleagues. You leverage your reputation—you borrow from your social and professional capital—to advocate for your colleague's professional advancement and growth.

Your colleague may need:

- Help with developing a key relationship with another colleague.
- A new position that takes advantage of their experience.
- Resources to accomplish their goals.
- A seat on an influential committee.

All of these are opportunities for you to step up and sponsor your colleague.

It is not enough to teach, mentor, coach, and supervise. Effective leaders also schedule focused time and energy to support, champion, and promote colleagues.

NOW WHAT?

Make a list of three individuals you will focus on sponsoring over the next month. How will you sponsor them? Who will you contact? How will your sponsorship create opportunities for them? When specifically will you do this?

Wear Multiple Hats

Effective leaders wear several different leadership hats during a one-to-one conversation. They adjust their tactics and approach depending on the perceived developmental needs of their colleague in the moment.

Jules had another opportunity to meet with his colleague who was experiencing burnout. He realized in his previous conversation that he had focused on mentoring and supervising. He had overplayed his expertise, and in response, his colleague had stopped listening.

This time Jules wore multiple leadership hats, and he genuinely felt that he had helped.

Jules began the conversation by wearing the coaching hat. He asked his colleague questions about burnout. He asked whether they had experienced burnout before, what they had done previously, and how they had seen others successfully overcome burnout. At times Jules clicked on a phrase to further illuminate his colleague's experience. He listened carefully to the answers and repeated key points back to help frame the conversation.

Then Jules saw an opportunity to teach, which his colleague welcomed. Jules taught about burnout trends within their industry, and shared information from a well-being group that suggested specific steps to move back toward well-being.

Jules then put the coaching hat back on to hear what his colleague was thinking about the new information and whether it was helpful.

Next, Jules sensed an opportunity to share his personal experience with burnout. He put on the mentoring hat. He shared his experience and relayed a story about a friend who seemed to have had a similar experience. Again, he followed this with a few coaching questions to get a sense of how his colleague would like to move forward.

His colleague cited a few factors that might be contributing to burnout. First, they felt isolated in the startup. They no longer had an opportunity to work closely with colleagues in their area of interest. And second, they thought that they were spending too much time in low-priority meetings, which were extending their workdays and preventing them from accomplishing needed tasks.

Jules put on the supervisor hat. He freed up his colleague's schedule by eliminating many of the low-priority meetings and re-prioritized some tasks. These changes opened much-needed focus time in his colleague's schedule.

While wearing the coaching hat earlier in the conversation, Jules had learned about an influential industry group forming a consortium to develop standards in an area of their technical expertise. Jules didn't mention it at the time, but the consortium's leader was an old colleague of his.[8] Jules put on his sponsor hat and gave that leader a call to recommend that his current colleague have a seat at the table. This workgroup would provide his colleague an opportunity to mix with other professionals in their area of expertise. It would also help the company maintain its compliance and agility with the evolving technical standards.

Finally, Jules put on the coaching hat and asked his colleague if it would be helpful to meet again in a few weeks. They could catch up and see how things were going. His colleague agreed.

A colleague is experiencing burnout and seeks your help. Which of the Five Hats of Effective Leaders would you wear?	
TEACH	"The data shows that 55 percent of our colleagues experience burnout."
	"This book notes that stress plus rest are essential for personal growth."
	"Psychological well-being is made up of the following six domains . . ."

MENTOR	"I too have experienced burnout, and this is how I approached it . . ." "You need to stop _____ and start _____." "Based upon what I have seen in other colleagues, I think you stay the course, and this will pass."
COACH	"What are your thoughts about how to best approach this?" "What would happen if you changed nothing in your approach?" "On one hand, you say *this*, and on the other, you say *that*. How do you reconcile those different thoughts?" "What are your next steps?"
SUPERVISOR	"Given what is occurring, I will recommend to the executive committee that we *make this change*." "I am going to decrease your time doing *this* and increase your time doing *that*." "We will hire a professional coach to help you . . ."
SPONSOR	"We need to use your talents better, and I will champion your efforts with *this influential person* to try to get you the resources you need." "I will recommend you for *this committee* in *this area of your interest*."

What's Next?

In this chapter we focused on one-to-one conversations. You learned how to wear the five hats of teacher, mentor, coach, supervisor, and sponsor. Part Two of this book delves into the ROW Forward Framework, which facilitates change in complex environments.

Executive Summary

➤ The Five Hats of Effective Leaders will help you have more effective one-to-one conversations with colleagues.

➤ The Five Hats of Effective Leaders are teacher, mentor, coach, supervisor, and sponsor. Each hat represents a different approach and uses a different tactic to help your colleague develop their skills, behaviors, and reasoning.

➤ When you teach, you convey new information and skills. You reveal knowledge previously unknown. And as you impart knowledge, you open new ways for your colleague to interpret their experiences.

➤ Your colleagues may not understand how and when to apply what they have learned. Colleagues also have fears and worries that restrict their application of knowledge and skills.

➤ When you mentor, you help your colleague envision the world through your experienced eyes. You are a subject matter expert. And as your colleague relays their experiences, you have an instinct of what might occur, what you would do, and how they might move forward.

➤ Your own blind spots limit the effectiveness of mentoring and whether your colleague finds your perspectives helpful. Mentoring may also inhibit your colleague from developing the ability to make their own decisions.

➤ When you coach, you help your colleague make sense of the world based on their own experiences, perspectives, and beliefs—through their own eyes. While wearing the coaching hat, you put aside your subject-matter expertise, and you view *your colleague as the expert* of their own experience. You ask open-ended questions to promote reflection and reframing.

➤ The GROW model provides a helpful sequence of themes for open-ended questions. You help your colleague understand their goal, the reality of the circumstances, the options for moving forward, and how they will achieve their goal.

➤ Each of us has specific phrases we use to speed up the flow of our thoughts and conversations. These words serve as shorthand—an abbreviated code—of our deeper thoughts and perspectives. When you "click on" a phrase, you investigate the meaning behind the words your colleagues use.

➤ When you supervise, you oversee your colleagues, your team, and your organization's day-to-day and long-term effectiveness. You identify and direct the removal of obstacles. You ensure that strategic goals are accomplished. You champion mission and values. You configure your team to work at its best.

➤ When a leader overplays supervision, they become overly prescriptive and impose their solutions on colleagues. They stifle the development of shared perspectives and shared adaptation.

➤ When you sponsor a colleague, you use your influence and connections to find opportunities for your colleague. It is essential that you leverage your reputation—that you expend your social and professional capital—to advocate for your colleagues.

➤ Effective leaders wear several different leadership hats during a one-to-one conversation. They adjust their tactics and approach depending on the perceived developmental needs of their colleague at the moment.

PART TWO

LEAD IN COMPLEX SITUATIONS

7

ROW FORWARD

Complex situations are those in which leaders most wonder, "Now what?" You meet a challenge too big to grasp, team members are frustrated, and you need to do something different. You sense the enveloping uncertainty and acknowledge the limitations of expertise as you proactively consider a change in approach.

Or you get unexpectedly stumped in the middle of a leadership moment—perhaps while presenting at a gathering or talking to your team or giving instructions. When you look at your colleagues, you realize that something has gone wrong. You have missed something significant. Instead of getting nods and looks of attention and engagement, you look out into a sea of negative emotions or blank stares. You're not in sync—and things are not going according to plan. The situation is both confused and complex, and you had failed to sense it.

My Unfortunate Event

I led several organizations in California before I moved back to Minnesota in 2015 to work at Mayo Clinic. When I arrived, my new boss asked me if I would serve as chair of finance for our twenty-one emergency departments. She wasn't sure what this would entail—Mayo had never had a chair of finance in the emergency department before. But it seemed like a good idea and it fit with my background, so when she asked me I said yes. I saw it as an opportunity to share knowledge.

As the first meeting approached, I prepared thoroughly. My

agenda was clear and detailed. I had a purpose, I made sure we would have time for discussion, and I had information, information, information. I was expecting a meeting in which there would be great discussion and forward movement.

It didn't work out that way.

I was allotted twenty minutes to talk about the effects of a physician's documentation on revenue. Each time a physician cares for a patient, they document the care provided. They write about the patient's history, the physical exam, the tests they order, and their decision-making process. Our physicians excel at this aspect of documentation, which is essential to providing great care. However, there also are parts of the documentation that are required for billing. And at times, those elements have little direct effect on the patient's care. I had identified opportunities to improve the documentation of those tedious billing details.

I expected that getting through this material in twenty minutes would be easy. I was an experienced presenter. No worries.

I went into the meeting in high spirits. This was my area of expertise. I saw an opportunity to open everyone's eyes with objective data, and I imagined that then we'd all drive great, empowering change together.

The meeting started as meetings usually do. We went over the agenda. I recall that we first talked about a scheduling tool, and then we discussed an improved stroke care protocol. Then it was my turn.

I dove right into it. I'd sorted the revenue data for each care encounter into five levels. There were three pages of tables. Each row had a different colleague's name in the left column; in the right columns were each physician's level of documentation. I handed out the information for everyone to see. I was being transparent.

My colleagues began looking at their numbers and seeing how they ranked. And they were seeing their personal statistics at that very moment, in the meeting, for the first time. And then they compared their results with the data of other colleagues in the room.

All of a sudden, the room changed. I noticed first that some smiles disappeared. I noticed next that there were several people in the room who were visibly angry or distraught. I could see a large vein bulging right in the middle of one colleague's forehead. Some colleagues had tears in their eyes. This was not what I had envisioned.

As I stood at the front of the room, I saw my brief career at Mayo Clinic flash before my eyes. I had just uprooted my family—my wife, teenage daughters, and our German shepherd—to move from California to Minnesota and I was bombing, big time. I, the middle-aged new guy, had just upset my colleagues—colleagues who had the power to promote me or let me go. I, the empathetic coach leader, had just ripped apart the well-being of my friends. Nice job, Richard.

And I thought to myself, "Now what?"

What Would You Do?

What would you have done in that moment?

Perhaps, on reflection, your first thought is, "That was dumb. I would never put myself or my colleagues in that situation. Who is this guy? And why am I reading his book?"

I know. I get that.

But let's get back to the initial question. Imagine you were me in that moment. Perhaps you've experienced a moment just like this during your career. What would you have done in this situation?

Run away? Of course! I've seen this technique used by leaders many times. Rather than acknowledge and understand the discomfort of the room, some leaders run away from the uneasiness as if it had never occurred. They continue on with the meeting. They hope their colleagues forget the upsetting moment ever took place. Next on the agenda, please.

On the contrary, perhaps you do the opposite. You don't run; rather, you dig in.

You explain. Each. Detail. Again. Because your colleagues obviously do not get it.

I call this the cognitive headlock. Some leaders face their confused, mad, sad audience and say—and I'm paraphrasing here: "Oh, I get it, I see that you're angry and that you're sad, but you don't have my expertise. I know this data's important and it's going to empower you. You disagree, but that's because you don't get it." And then they double down. They reassert why their data is important. They rationalize to themselves that they just need to teach their colleagues and show them where they are wrong. The leader thinks they just need to make it happen and eventually their colleagues will catch up to them and thank them. The leader. The expert.

The cognitive headlock is used by leaders in all industries. It's a decision by the leader to simply push through resistance, employing their expertise and power against their colleagues. They demonstrate entrained thinking as they stifle the autonomy of others.

Neither the cognitive headlock nor running away are good strategies when dealing with complex challenges. There is a better way.

NOW WHAT?

Think about a recent confused meeting you have attended. How did you or your colleagues jump to options and the way forward before discovering the shared reality of the room?

Consider how you might apply the ROW Forward framework moving forward.

The ROW Forward Framework

It's helpful to have a sequence of steps to follow as you think through complex challenges and create action. Throughout the rest of the book, you will be introduced to the individual steps of the ROW Forward framework.

Over the past seven years of leading, coaching, and consulting at Mayo Clinic, I've developed this model to help leaders and their teams quickly come together around the tangled, uncomfortable, complex issues they face. In developing the ROW Forward framework, I incorporated elements of the one-to-one coaching model—the GROW model—that we discussed in Chapter Six, and created a framework to help leaders effectively facilitate—to coach—large groups of colleagues as they work through complex challenges.

The framework guides a process that is adaptable to your situation. It can be applied in a matter of minutes or it may provide the approach for a multi-day retreat. You may use it in solitude, in partnership with your executive team, or broadly to leverage the wisdom of your entire organization.

The ROW Forward framework consists of the following three steps, which may then be repeated:

1. Construct Shared **Reality** and direction.

2. Generate multiple **Options**.

3. Identify the **Way Forward** and create action.

4. Repeat the **ROW Forward**.

ROW Forward Framework

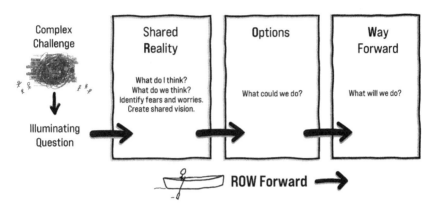

Here is a summary of the framework.

Create Shared Reality

During the first phase of the ROW Forward process, you develop shared reality to bring together your perceptions with the perceptions of colleagues. In leveraging combined—and often divergent—insights, you develop collective wisdom about complex challenges.

To create shared reality, you:

Document your perspectives. Define what you think about the complex challenge. Spell out your perspectives of the strengths, weaknesses, opportunities, threats, fears, and worries as they relate to the complex challenge.

Create shared reality. Each member of your team has their own perspectives of the complex challenge—and their own blind spots. Facilitate the creation of shared reality to collectively consider how you and your colleagues make sense of the complex world.

Identify fears and worries. Fears and worries operate like subconscious monsters in our heads. They prevent individual and organizational goal attainment. Discover fears and worries and add them to the shared reality.

Create shared vision. Draft a shared vision to address how you and your colleagues will proceed. Ensure that your vision aligns with the mission and core values of the organization. Address the fears and worries you will work to defuse.

Generate Multiple Options

During the second phase of the ROW Forward process, you generate multiple options for what you might do as you move forward.

Single options stifle us. We learn from researchers like Paul Nutt that the more options we have, the greater the likelihood of success. Yet far too many organizations use an *either this or that* single option model. That may seem efficient, but it has a higher likelihood of failure. The ROW Forward framework puts an emphasis on generating multiple options and brainstorming possibilities. Even crazy ideas—the ones you would never implement—can stimulate the creation of better options to pursue.

Pick the options to pursue. Explore the pros and cons of each prospective option. Choose three to five options to pursue from the long list of potential options. Each of these options becomes an objective as you consider your best way forward.

Champion the Way Forward

During the final phase of the ROW Forward process, move to action
to achieve results as your way forward.

Identify objectives and key results (OKRs). Each objective
represents an option you have chosen to pursue. For each
objective, define key results that describe how you will know
you have met each objective.

Identify the directly responsible individual (DRI). Identify a
single accountable individual to be directly responsible for
each way forward. The DRI is the steward for each task. They
protect and feed the task. They ensure that the team meets
and that the tasks are accomplished.

Choose the objective team (OT). Each objective has a team of
individuals assigned to work with the DRI to ensure that
each objective and key result is achieved. Generally, OTs are
best kept small—from two to five individuals.

Address scheduling. Decide when you'll start each option,
where and how often you will meet, and when you will
report back with your findings to the larger group.

Delegate. When delegating a task you need to consider what you
are specifically delegating and how well you know the competency of the individual assigned to each task. Delegate at
one of three levels based upon your level of trust and familiarity with each colleague: check box, consider and recommend, or complete levels of delegation.

The way forward. Learn fast and fail fast. Share your findings
with colleagues. Consider each objective and key result to
be an experiment—a hypothesis to be tested. As you pursue
each way forward you may encounter resistance, and you

may encounter success or failure. As you proceed, you probe the complex environment and then feed what is learned back into your evolving shared reality.

Time and Scope

It's important to consider how much time you have and the scope of the diverse perspectives you will involve in the ROW Forward process. The more time and the broader your scope, and the more diversity of opinions you gather as part of the decision-making process—the more wisdom you will create.

But what if you don't have a lot of time?

A message of this book is *not* that you need to hold multi-day retreats for each complex situation that arises. That is not realistic. You are surrounded by complexity, and there are not enough hours in a day to dissect each ambiguity. However, it's clear that you don't want to simply wing it based upon your expertise without some discipline for deeper investigation. There is a middle ground.

The ROW Forward process adapts to your situation. There will be times when the clock ticks fast or the topic is too sensitive, and you need to rely on a smaller set of colleagues with a tighter time frame to make a decision. But there will also be occasions when your timeline is less pressured, and you have more options.

Which colleagues participate in the search for shared reality will often hinge on your timeline. Not every situation can be addressed by organizing a retreat, but some warrant that level of attention. You'll need to make that call. It will also depend upon who is most affected by the outcome of the inquiry. You want those voices to be heard now, not when you implement a solution that those affected groups can't abide.

ROW Forward with a Few Colleagues

As you run the list of to-dos and douse fires with your colleagues, you may encounter a complex issue that requires you to pause and take a half-hour to step up to the balcony to quickly consider the situation and your options for action. A brief moment on the balcony may be all it takes, or that may be a first step before opening up the illuminating question to others.

ROW Forward with a Large Team

There are times when you bring together larger numbers of individuals, such as a workgroup, a board of trustees, or a committee to consider a complex decision. This tactic is commonly used during meetings or retreats.

ROW Forward an Organization

There are times when an organization may invoke the ROW Forward framework to promote cultural alignment, to create long-term strategy, and to maximize cooperative efforts during times of tremendous opportunity and change. The ROW Forward framework provides a common language and structure to facilitate organizational thinking, communication, and action. This process harnesses the wisdom of distributed expertise and promotes both decentralization and agility in decision-making.

ROW Forward Alone

Highly effective leaders routinely take time to step up to the balcony. The mere act of deliberately considering other perspectives helps develop wisdom; it's certainly better than reflexively deciding while complex scenarios unfold all around them.

There are times when, by necessity, you need to process a situation alone rather than discuss it with colleagues. Perhaps the issue is too personal, or adversarial, or you have not yet established a network of trusted individuals. During these times, you may choose to ROW Forward alone.

Be careful, though, when you go it alone. You may be tempted to simply cling to your own sense of reality and avoid pursuing shared reality. It may seem that working alone saves time, but in fact, it may set you up for a long, arduous process later. When you work alone, you may miss or underestimate key perspectives. It is often better to use the ROW Forward process to bring colleagues together around contentious issues.

Investing this time upfront can allay discomfort, increase trust as you share perspectives, and improve efficiency moving forward. Wading into what is uncomfortable and unsaid may defuse perceptions of difference and improve the likelihood of success. Some of your fears about involving others may be due to inexperience in leading in complexity and a worry about opening up discord. We will address how to respond to these very sensible fears, and how to facilitate sharing in a way that maximizes the safety of all involved.

Additionally, if you have the option during these times of isolation, your effectiveness could be improved if you seek the services of a coach or the help of an outside peer—an individual who has no specific agenda related to your decision who could help you look around blind spots. Consider calling a mentor or a confidant from another organization to help you process the issues.

ROW Forward Framework

Alone

A Few Colleagues

A Large Team

An Organization

How Long Does Each Step of ROW Forward Take?

As a rule of thumb, reserve 70 percent of the available time to create shared reality, 20 percent to identify multiple options for how to move forward, and 10 percent to plan the way forward. Therefore, if two hours are available, I may allot one hour and twenty minutes to document shared reality, twenty-five minutes to generate options, and fifteen minutes to navigate a way forward.

NOW WHAT?

How does the ROW Forward framework compare to your usual approach to decision-making when facing complex challenges?

A Typical Confused Meeting

Remember the ROW Forward framework as you sit in your next confused meeting. A complex issue will be discussed, and you and your colleagues will skip the creation of shared reality. Some think the solution is clear and you just need to continue with best practice. Some see that the problem is a complicated issue and believe that expert opinion will provide the best guidance.

When you and your colleagues skip the development of shared reality, you jump to options or a way forward. You hear statements of individual expertise: "We need to do this." "That is not an option." "That is incorrect." "They will never support this." You note verbal and nonverbal cues of heightened emotions. Your colleagues express anger and sadness. Some get louder, others become quiet, and some stare blankly in a state of dissociation. And in this confused space, you realize that a different and more coherent process is needed.

Let's go back to the unfortunate event described earlier in this chapter. When I presented transparent finance data to my colleagues in the emergency department, I skipped the development of shared reality and jumped to options and the way forward. I unlocked the confused state.

Some colleagues thought the data should never have been presented transparently. Some didn't know why it was presented. Some thought we should have just helped individuals improve their results. There were different interpretations of what the data meant and why it was being presented. Some felt that discussing finance was an assault on the culture and the mission of the organization. Many were concerned about how this would affect the finances of their patients. It was confused and it was messy, and I took us there quickly.

This is not to say that confused meetings are necessarily caused by the leader. There are times, despite the best intentions, when what has been simmering and unsaid is brought to a boil. These are times when the views of the formal network, with its hierarchy and titles, and the informal network, with its loose matrix of relationships, come together. We each have different perspectives and experiences, and sometimes it takes a moment of confusion to open up the opportunity to explore complexity. The confusion makes the need to change palpable. And it is an opportunity that should not be wasted.

So, what next? What did we do?

There was no cognitive headlock. There was no running away. I paused and took the pulse of the room. I recognized the confusion and asked my colleagues to share what they were thinking and feeling.

Then, we scheduled time to meet together to create shared reality. And then, only after we created shared reality, did we move to generate multiple options. And then, after generating options, we adopted ways forward. We moved sequentially through the ROW Forward framework.

What's Next?

In the following chapters you will learn how to apply each step of the ROW Forward framework. Additionally, you will begin to recognize the common fears and behaviors that may threaten to upset the process and show you how to lead through those difficulties.

Executive Summary

➤ The ROW Forward framework guides your decision-making process in complex situations.

➤ Each step of ROW Forward is to be done sequentially.

➤ Individuals and organizations have different expertise, perceptions, and experiences. Develop shared reality to leverage and develop collective wisdom around the complex issue.

➤ Generate multiple options for what you might do in response to the complex problem.

➤ Choose a few options to pursue as a way forward. Ensure that you have assigned directly responsible individuals (DRIs), organized objective teams (OTs), have specific timelines with metrics, and have a way to communicate findings and results.

➤ Confused meetings signal that you may be considering a decision from the complex domain. Moving to ROW Forward will help you engage colleagues around developing effective solutions.

➤ The ROW Forward model adjusts to the time available and the desired scope of your process. You may ROW Forward with a few colleagues, in groups, as organizations, or alone. And you may do so in a matter of minutes or over a several-day retreat.

➤ A rule of thumb is to allot 70 percent of the time available for the ROW Forward process to the development of shared reality, 20 percent to generating potential options for action, and 10 percent to defining the specific actions to pursue as a way forward.

8

DOCUMENT YOUR PERSPECTIVES

ROW Forward Framework

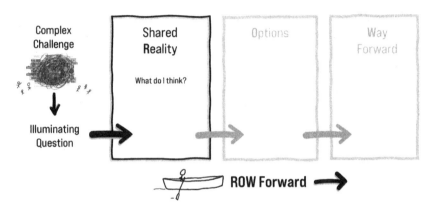

The creation of shared reality brings together your perspectives of a complex challenge with the perspectives of your colleagues.

Your Perspectives
+ Their Perspectives
Shared Reality

The first step in creating shared reality requires that you understand your own perspectives of the complex challenge. You need to move beyond your reflexive instincts about what is going on and how you would immediately approach the issues and make sense of the situation in a more deliberate and thoughtful manner. You need to get off the dance floor and step up to the balcony to consider the challenge with a broader perspective. And as you take the time to deliberately consider the situation, you give yourself an opportunity to look past some of your own blind spots.

There are six steps to move from the dance floor up to the balcony. An effective leader:

1. Creates time and space to think.

2. Identifies a complex problem.

3. Captures their own thoughts.

4. Expands their perspectives.

5. Identifies themes.

6. Body swaps.

An important caveat as we proceed: There are times when you only have a few minutes to step up to the balcony, while at other times you have weeks to consider an issue. Additionally, there are times when only you can step up to the balcony, but at other times you can engage colleagues to join in. Don't fret these limitations. In Chapter Nine we will discuss how you can flex the ROW Forward framework to adapt to your specific situation.

Create Time and Space to Think

As you consider complex issues, it's essential that you create time and space to think about them. Many of us are so used to working on the fly, putting out fires, and leveraging our expertise in the moment that we need to be reminded of the importance of deep, uninterrupted thought. As busy people, we tend to equate productivity with action. Action is important, but preparative thinking is essential to ensure that busy times are focused and productive when facing volatile, uncertain, ambiguous situations. Complex problems require deliberate and concentrated thought.

Carve Out a Time Ritual

In his short story "Harrison Bergeron," Kurt Vonnegut wrote about a society of the future in which everyone is mandated to be equal. Those deemed to be above average are required to wear handicapping devices.[1] Those with good looks are required to wear rubber noses, those who move with grace are required to wear unbalanced pieces of jagged heavy metal, and those of higher intelligence are required to wear earpieces that emit loud jarring sounds at irregular intervals to interrupt thought.

In modern society, the imagined future is already here—at least with respect to the thought-blocking devices that envelop us. Your thoughts may be interrupted by emails, messages, in-person interruptions, calendar events, and social media. And with each interruption, your opportunity to have deep thoughts decreases. But you are not required to nurture or to invite these interruptions. You can carve out time to think.

The leaders I coach use many different approaches to secure time for deep thought. Some schedule specific times on specific days each week for thinking. Others have morning or nighttime rituals during which they journal and process their day. Some instruct their assistants to block chunks of time with appointments labeled "Deep Work" or "[Insert topic here] Strategy" for deep thought. Regardless of the method employed, the most effective leaders I coach deliberately block time for deep thinking. It is not left to chance. That open spot on your calendar on Wednesday at 1 p.m., the one you were going to use for deep thinking, will be filled by someone else's priority if you don't reserve the time for yourself. Create a time ritual for deep thinking.

Adopt a Constraint Ritual

But carving out time for thought is not enough. You also need to create the space—the atmosphere—for uninterrupted thought. Deep thought requires isolation from the disruption of social media, emails, messages, phone calls, and colleagues walking in to ask you "just one quick question."[2] Deep thinking requires a target-like focus on the complex issue—a silencing of distracting thoughts. You need to prevent the reflexive urge to search the Internet for that one tangential thing that pops into your mind. Productive thought requires constraints.

I have my own personal constraint ritual for deep thought:

- I make a cup of Longjing green tea brewed at the perfect temperature with osmotically filtered water.
- I close the door and set a timer, which keeps me in my chair.
- I keep an index card nearby so I can capture and put aside the occasional tangential thought (*which word describes the smell of rain?*).

- I wear noise-canceling headphones for quiet, and to alert others that I am not to be disturbed.
- I listen to silence, or when there are distracting noises, I listen to unfocused low-volume ambient music by Max Richter or Brian Eno.
- I open a writing application, quit other distracting applications, and silence all notifications.

Many thinkers go to solitary locations of retreat to do their best work. While I do not have an isolated cabin in the woods for deep thought, I find that once I put on the headphones and block out the world, I have generous headspace in which to think. And this undisturbed place for deep thought is both predictable and accessible, whether in my office, at home, or on a plane—I have a portable ritual that triggers productive thinking.

Once you create time and space to think on the balcony, identify the complex problem you will consider.

NOW WHAT?

What actions will you take to carve out the time and space needed to consider your complex issue? When specifically will your deep thinking occur? What constraint rituals will you employ?

Identify a Complex Challenge

On the second step up to the balcony, you identify a complex challenge to consider.

Complex challenges come in many different forms. Some involve hard-to-grasp, future-focused plans, whereas others focus on real-time issues needing immediate direction. For example, will you focus on how to develop a long-term strategy for your organization? Or will you focus on how you might change the staffing schedule to accommodate current business needs? Both of these—future-focused issues and real-time issues—can be addressed from the balcony perspective of the ROW Forward framework (construct shared reality, generate multiple options, and identify the way forward). And often, addressing one will help the other.

Sometimes you choose the complex issue as it rises to the top of your mind. At other times you work with your colleagues to pick the issue the team chooses to tackle in the moment.

Muhammad Ali is quoted as having said, "It isn't the mountains ahead that wear you out; it's the pebble in your shoe." Some of the most effective leaders with whom I work conduct "pebble in your shoe" meetings on a quarterly or semi-annual basis. They ask their colleagues to help them identify the next complex issue to tackle. "What are the pebbles in your shoe?" "What are the frustrating, time-consuming things that get in your way?"

And from these conversations they choose a pebble to remove from the shoe. They stand on the balcony and apply ROW Forward thinking to improve the effectiveness of their work environment.

Test for Complexity

But how can you be sure that what you're considering is a complex, rather than just a complicated or a chaotic issue? You become aware of a complex challenge by sensing that what you're doing now is not working or will not work as you move forward. Then, you ask and answer the following questions:

1. Does it seem that best practices (also known as past practices) no longer work?

2. Does this seem like a messy problem in which there are many different opinions and no clear predictable outcomes?

3. Do your colleagues disagree on which variables are import- ant to consider?

If you answered yes to these three questions, the challenge is neither clear nor complicated. If the challenge was clear, you would use established best practices to solve it. If the challenge was compli- cated, you would ask the experts. Therefore, the challenge is either complex or chaotic.

To figure this out, you ask a fourth question:

4. Do you have time to consider your approach to the problem?

If the answer to question four is no, there is not time to consider it, the challenge is chaotic, and you need to make decisions quickly from the dance floor. If the answer is yes, you have time to consider your approach, and the challenge is complex.

Craft an Illuminating Question

You read about several examples of complex challenges in the intro- duction of this book:

*   The hospital CEO asked, "How might we work with the cardiology group to strengthen partnership and consider options that will be mutually beneficial?"
*   The product manager asked, "How do we bring the tech- nology team and the marketing team together to establish a collaborative workflow?"
*   The academic chair asked, "How do we respect the current

power structures and leverage the traditional processes, yet move forward with bold and forward thinking?"

- The chief human resource officer asked, "How do we retain top talent and maintain healthy margins during challenging financial times?"

Note that the complex challenge is best described in the form of a question. And the question is formulated using the following rules:

- It is stated in the positive.
- It has a future focus.
- It implicates you.

State the question in the positive to plot an opportunity, rather than to avoid an obstacle. "How do we become better skiers?" is, for example, much better than "How do we avoid that tree? Don't hit that tree. Don't hit that tree!" Strategize toward positive outcomes, not away from the disastrous results.

Look to where you want to go using a future focus, rather than examining the past. We do not drive forward looking in the rearview mirror. We look to the road ahead. We focus on what we want to occur in the future, we focus on the risks ahead, we focus on the opportunities in front of us.

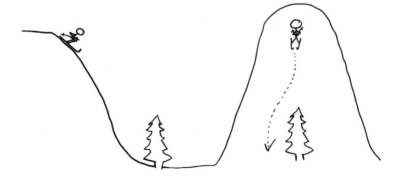

Choose opportunities and embrace challenges that directly involve you—the ones you have the power to change. You cannot change a colleague, or make your competition do something else. But you can figure out how you might effectively influence each of them. Reframe your thinking from "My challenge is those engineers; they need to change" to "How can I best influence the engineers?" Make sure your illuminating question implicates you and your team.

NOW WHAT?

What complex issue will you consider?

- Does it seem that best practices (also known as past practices) no longer work?

- Does this seem like a messy problem in which there are many different opinions and no clear predictable outcomes?

- Do your colleagues disagree on which variables are important to consider?

- Do you have time to consider your approach to the problem?

- State your illuminating question in the positive, with a future focus framed in a manner that implicates you.

Capture Your Thoughts in Written Form

Now that you've chosen the illuminating question, it's time to capture your thoughts about the question being considered.

It is essential to capture your thinking in written form as you construct your model of the complex dance floor. We attend many meetings and have wonderful hallway conversations during which great ideas and different perspectives are exchanged and then lost because they have not been captured. We also get stuck perseverating about the same parts of an issue, over and over again. Writing down our thinking disentangles us from this avoidable trap.

Your thoughts are not songs on the dance floor that vanish once played. Rather, your thoughts are bits of precious data—pieces of a multidimensional puzzle—to be captured, documented, and then examined from all sides. When you stand on the balcony, you connect these pieces to create a diorama-like model of the dance floor: you create a model of thinking. Later, when you share your model with colleagues, they have an opportunity to track your thinking and to add alternate perspectives and angles. Then, together, you may expand the model of the complex world.

Each thought, each point of view, about the illuminating question is to be written as a bullet point; a single nugget of data. You have a sense of what is occurring, the opportunities available, the risks and limitations, and how things might evolve as you ponder the illuminating question. Write those thoughts down.

One of the departments within Mayo Clinic was trying to figure out an illuminating question: "How do we expand the use of telemedicine to meet the needs of our patients?"

Here are examples of the initial bullets written for this question by one leader:

- Telemedicine allows patients access to care from almost anywhere.
- A physical exam over video is limited (e.g., cannot listen to the heart).
- Patients may not be familiar with the technology.
- Our electronic health record is not configured for a telemedicine evaluation.

- Many healthcare organizations are successfully employing telemedicine.
- Some older physicians are not comfortable with the technology.
- May hinder the physician-patient relationship.
- We don't know whether patients will like it.
- How do we get vital signs?

As you can imagine, the list grew quite lengthy, as there were many things to consider. And notice that there was no specific pattern this individual followed as they initially wrote down their thoughts. They emptied their mind of whatever thoughts arose in the moment. This initial unconstrained process of brainstorming— writing whatever comes to mind—is important. Initially, you just let your thoughts emerge. As you sit quietly in deep thought, the entries will arise. There is no need for editing or categorizing yet; that occurs during a later step.

Tools to Capture Your Thoughts

There are several ways you can capture your thinking in written form.

Paper, whiteboard, and chalkboards are often easily available. Because they are unplugged—not digital—you may be less prone to being distracted by notifications. You simply pick up a pen or pencil or piece of chalk and write down each thought as a bullet point.

Sticky notes and notecards have the advantage of being both unplugged and having just the right amount of space to capture a single thought. You can stick them to a desk, a wall, or any other flat surface. Later it will be easy to edit and move your thoughts around into themes.

Mind-mapping, outlining software, writing applications, and other technology tools provide speedy capture and also have the advantage of allowing you to easily move ideas and group them into themes. Their electronic nature also makes it easy to save, reproduce, and print.

We will talk later about more advantages and disadvantages for each of these technologies as we discuss specific examples of ways in which you can facilitate large group discussion. For example, how do you facilitate a complex discussion when emotions are on edge and trust is challenged? The method by which you capture the thinking of a contentious group carries the possibility of either hurting or helping the process.

NOW WHAT?

What technology will you use to capture your thoughts?

What rituals, applications, and processes are your colleagues using to improve their effectiveness?

Subscribe to my newsletter to see an updated list of the technologies, rituals, and processes I use to improve leadership effectiveness. You can sign up at richardwinters.com/newsletter

Expand Your Perspective

After you've made the initial effort of emptying your mind, it's time to expand your perspective. This can be done by deliberately using questions as prompts. There are many ways to approach this process, and there is no single correct combination of questions. A best practice is to write several responses for each question. As you write each successive answer, you broaden your perspective. You discover nuance.

What do **you think** is going on?

1.	11.	21.
2.	12.	22.
3.	13.	23.
4.	14.	24.
5.	15.	25.
6.	16.	26.
7.	17.	27.
8.	18.	28.
9.	19.	29.
10.	20.	30.

You could specifically ask yourself these questions:

- What are the opportunities?
- What are the risks and limitations?
- How might this situation evolve?
- What is the competition doing?
- How does this affect our customer?

After answering each question, ask yourself, "What else?" or "How else?" to probe deeper. For example:

- "What are the opportunities?" [you write a response]
- "What else? What are other opportunities?" [you write another response]

Or:

- How does this affect our customer? [you write a response]

- How else does this affect our customer? [you write another response]

Use the same pattern of asking "what else?" and "how else?" as follow-up for any of the questions introduced below.

You might use the well-known SWOT method, which asks:

- What are the strengths?
- What are the weaknesses?
- What are the opportunities?
- What are the threats?

And you could think specifically about other entities, people, and organizations involved in the complex issue. How does this affect your

- colleagues?
- supply chain?
- distributors?
- partners?

You might look at the different job descriptions within your organization and consider how key individuals might be affected:

- How does this affect other departments and divisions?
- How does this affect each of the individuals on our organizational chart?
- How does this affect job descriptions and recruiting needs?
- How does this affect our reporting structure?

You could employ the mnemonic PESTLE to consider the situation from macro-environmental perspectives:

- Political
- Economic
- Social
- Technological
- Legal
- Environmental

Finally, you might think about the issue from the perspective of different time frames.

How might the situation be different? What might change

- in one month?
- in one year?
- after this new hire occurs?
- during the summer?
- after a worldwide pandemic recedes?

Repeat the questioning process until you have met your allotted time, or you have nothing left to write—your mind has been emptied.

Identify Themes

Now that you have captured these thoughts, it's time to find themes in the ideas you've written. Then, once you have identified a theme, your next step is to group your bulleted thoughts into those themes.

Recall the question of how to expand telemedicine at Mayo Clinic. Amidst those initial bulleted thoughts, we notice possible themes. There may be a technology theme and a patient experience theme emerging from the data.

For example:

Technology

- Who will support the software for patients and physicians?
- There are many potential software vendors.
- Our electronic health record system is not configured for telemedicine evaluation.
- How do we fund the technology upgrades required?

Patient Experience

- Patients don't have to sit in the waiting room.
- Diminishes the risk of contagion.
- Allows patients access from anywhere.
- We don't know whether patients will like it.
- May hinder the physician-patient relationship.
- How about the patients who cannot afford the technology?

What do **you think** is going on?

Theme 1	Theme 2	Theme 3
1.	1.	1.
2.	2.	2.
3.	3.	3.
4.	4.	4.
5.	5.	5.
6.	6.	6.
7.	7.	7.
8.	8.	8.
9.		9.
10.		10.
11.		
12.		

As you begin to place bullets into themes, more thoughts will arise, and these perspectives should be added to the appropriate theme. You'll find that as you continue to explore themes, some of them may break into several subthemes or into new themes.

Again, there is no single correct way. At times a thought may fit into several possible themes. It's up to you whether you place it under one theme, or put it into several themes. You're the leader. Do whatever gives you the best perspective.

Body Swap

When I was a child, I went to see the movie *Freaky Friday* in the theater. The plot of the movie revolved around a mother and her daughter swapping bodies for a day. In this way, they experienced life from each other's perspective. Now, there is a whole genre of "body swap" movies: in *Face/Off*, an agent has a face transplant to assume the life a deceased criminal; in *Shrek the Third*, the Donkey and Puss in Boots swap cartoon bodies; and in *Yuen Mei Ching Yan*, a dog swaps bodies with a human. This is entertaining stuff.

As a leader, your ability to see things from the perspectives of others, to empathize, to body swap, will improve your efficacy in complex situations. It makes sense to carve out a moment or two to imagine what the complex situation looks like from the perspective of others.

What might things really look like from the perspective of your customer, your colleague, your competition? What are their opportunities? What are their fears and worries? What might they think of your actions? What do they see as they look out from their balcony?

Write your body swap thoughts down. Add these perspectives to the model of reality you're creating.

What's Next?

At this point, you can pat yourself on the back. You have pulled your-self out of the center of the action and stationed your thinking on a high balcony. You've discovered and clarified your thinking and, most importantly, documented it.

The well-considered document that now appears before you is your sense of the reality of the complex situation. The next step is to share your sense of reality—this model of the complex world—with your colleagues.

But before we proceed to the next step, we need to investigate some of the flaws—the blind spots—in your sense of reality. This is the topic of the next chapter.

Executive Summary

> ➤ Create the time and follow a deliberate process to examine your thinking about illuminating questions. Take time to step up from the dance floor to the balcony.

> ➤ Carve out time and space for uninterrupted thought. Establish constraint rituals.

> ➤ Identify a complex challenge, use the four-question test for complexity, and then frame the issue in the form of a positive, future-focused illuminating question that directly implicates you.

> ➤ Capture your thinking in written form using bullets for each thought.

> ➤ Expand your perspective by asking questions to discover different points of view about the complex issue. Follow up each question by asking "What else?" or "How else?" to expand perspective.

➤ Identify themes for the bulleted thoughts, and then collect each of the thoughts under a theme.

➤ Imagine your complex issue from the perspective of someone else using the body swap method. Then, add the imagined perspectives to your developing model of the world.

CREATE A SHARED REALITY

ROW Forward Framework

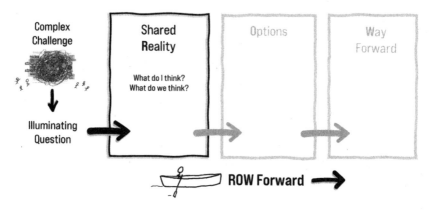

A smart fish swims along and encounters a wise fish swimming in the opposite direction, who nods and says, "Good morning. How's the water?" The smart fish swims on for a bit, and then wonders, "What is water?"[1]

Each fish is an expert swimmer. However, the smart fish lacks a crucial perspective. Within its framing of reality, the smart fish doesn't see the water. It's blind to the very thing that envelops it, that buoys it, that sustains it. It is too close to the water. It is subject to the water, and does not see itself as an object separate from the water. The smart fish is unaware, and it is unaware that it is unaware.

The wise fish, also an expert swimmer, sees what the smart fish has not. The wise fish views their large fishbowl from a different vantage point. It was once a smart fish until its own sense of reality was challenged, and it now realizes that it—a fish—is different from water. Perhaps, the smart fish, as it swims along, will consider the perspectives of the wise fish and challenge its own thinking.

Wisdom

Your effectiveness as a leader correlates directly with your ability to consider different perspectives—to develop wisdom. The wiser you become, the less enmeshed you are within your own perspective of the fishbowl.

As a leader develops wisdom, they consider ideas they may have once discarded as misinformed meanderings or careless contradictions. They see things less frequently as me versus them, my way versus their way, or what I do versus what they do, and their binary thoughts of "yes" or "no," and "this" or "that," evolve. They begin to see the oversimplification and inaccuracy of dichotomous forms of thinking. Instead, the wise leader thinks dialectically; they view issues from multiple different perspectives and understand that seemingly opposing views can both be true.[2] They become dissatisfied with simple, isolated black-and-white sketches of reality gripped by tight hands and prefer to develop shared portraits of rich, multicolored hues that reveal more detailed, yet complex, scenes.

Research shows us that a leader's ability to challenge existing processes, inspire shared vision, manage conflict, solve problems, delegate, empower, and build relationships correlates with their ability to challenge their own perspectives when they encounter complex decisions.[3] A wise leader may avoid taking sides. This isn't being wishy-washy. Instead, it's the leader demonstrating a greater depth of perspective. They see multiple paths, rather than a single path, and they see the pitfalls involved with each path more clearly. When a wise leader commits to action, they are more adept at predicting and noting problems as they arise. They adjust more effectively as situations change.

In Chapter Three, you stepped up to the balcony (above the fishbowl) to document your sense of reality. Now it's time to challenge your perspectives in order to elevate your own wisdom as well as that of your colleagues and your organization.

The Wisdom of Your Crowd

The product manager has a perspective, as does each colleague on the technology and the marketing team. The chief human resource officer has a perspective, as does the CFO, the COO, and the CEO. The hospital CEO has a perspective, as does each physician in the cardiology group. And the wise leader—the wise product manager, chief human resource officer, and CEO—feels constrained, if not downright claustrophobic, in the fishbowl if they attempt to move forward in complexity without first seeking the insights and perspectives of their colleagues.

In his book *The Wisdom of Crowds*, James Surowiecki lists four conditions that characterize wise groups of individuals: diversity of opinion; opinions determined independently; members seeking the viewpoints of both local and external experts; and bringing those different perspectives together in making a decision.[4] As you continue reading this chapter, you will learn how to bring diverse groups of colleagues together to share independent opinions and expertise, helping you facilitate the creation of shared reality and empowering the formation of collective wisdom.

As you accomplish this step of the ROW Forward framework, you and your colleagues step up from individual sketches of reality—blind spots and all—to a nuanced and shared portrait of reality. Your team will develop a wisdom that enhances its capacity to adjust, reframe, and take action in volatile, uncertain, complex, and ambiguous environments.

Diverse Opinions

Diversity is necessary for wise decision-making: Diversity of thought, background, and experience.

Effective leaders surround themselves with diverse working groups of colleagues. These workgroups exchange viewpoints and challenge each other's perspectives. The CEO, COO, and CFO; the project manager, technology director, and marketing director; the academic department chair and a few divisional chairs—effective leadership teams bring out the best in each other through a process of respectful challenges.

Mayo Clinic relies on diverse leadership triads to make decisions.[5] Each triad includes a physician leader, a nursing leader, and an administrative leader.[6] For example, in the Department of Emergency Medicine, the physician chair of emergency medicine, the emergency nursing director, and the emergency operations administrator work together to make decisions. Imagine the diversity of perspectives that an administrator, a physician, and a nurse bring to a complex situation. They fact-check each other. They expand on each other's simple stories before moving to action. The physician leader asks, "Am I seeing this correctly?" The nursing or administrative leader responds, "Um, that is one perspective. This, on the other hand, is what we experience."

Numerous studies reveal the importance of diversity in effective decision-making. Diverse ages, genders, races, and ethnicities within executive teams, for example, function as competitive differentiators that improve such things as financial return, innovation, fact-finding, objectivity, and, as it so happens, decision-making when compared to the results of homogeneous teams.[7, 8, 9, 10, 11] This makes sense. When your team is composed of people who think like you, look like you, and talk like you, they most likely agree with you, which means that your thinking may lack critical perspective.

Homogeneous groups of individuals have similar blind spots, and as a result, their framing of the complex world is impoverished. The complex space is diverse, and it stands to reason that diversity of experience and thought are essential elements for organizations that want to better navigate such environments (i.e., the VUCA world). Effective teams are diverse teams.

How Do You Facilitate Diversity of Opinion?

There are several effective ways . . .

Create Teams with Diversity in Mind

Look at your team. Do you have opportunities to improve the diversity of the skills, experience, profession, age, gender, race, and ethnicity represented in decision-making? Forward-thinking leaders hire and promote colleagues to enhance the diversity of perspectives. They recruit, measure, and invest in the creation of diverse teams.

Bring In Different Personality Traits

Seek out colleagues who experience and process the world in a manner that's different from yours. Are you an enthusiastic and imaginative visionary who loves to think about what is possible? Your decisions will be improved if you include the insights of someone who is quiet, focused, and orderly; someone who seeks to be grounded in the current reality. If the thought of being an enthusiastic and imaginative visionary is foreign to you, try to get a colleague with those personality traits on your team.

Welcome Disagreement

Look for those individuals who disagree with you. Ask a prospective team member, "Do you disagree? Good, welcome to the team."

Make Diverse Opinions Matter

Survey your colleagues, and ask them whether or not they think their opinions matter. In Chapter Five, we discussed how Mayo Clinic measures leadership behaviors through anonymous surveys of a leader's direct reports. One survey question specifically asks if the leader "encourages me to suggest ideas for improvement." When your colleagues disagree with this statement, you have an opportunity to improve the way you elicit your colleagues' diverse opinions.

Seek Divergent Perspectives

Gather information from third parties to help you bring divergent perspectives forward. Some sources to consider:

- Books
- Magazine articles
- Newspaper articles
- Blog posts
- Journal articles
- Social media
- Interviews with experts
- Podcasts
- Conferences

This is a good way for individuals to bring alternative points of view to the discussion without having to adopt each alternative as their own.

Independent Opinions

On any given day, I coach a leader who wants to talk more, and then during the very next session, I coach another leader who wants to speak less.

The leader who wants to talk more tends to be quiet; they keep their perspective to themselves during meetings, particularly contentious ones. Perhaps they need more time to think through issues, or they're concerned about upsetting others, or they simply think it is polite to be quiet while others contribute to the conversation. Conversely, the leader who wants to talk less, openly shares their perspectives during meetings about things both familiar to them and things they hear for the first time. Perhaps they think out loud, or they're concerned they will not be heard, or they sense their job as a leader is to repeatedly champion their perspective as others weigh in. Or perhaps nobody else is talking, so someone needs to fill the empty void of silence.

Now imagine how a talkative leader and a quiet one might interact in a meeting about a complex issue: Each leader has their own perspective, but more often than not, one leader shares, and the other withholds. This unilateral sharing of perspective is antagonistic to the development of wisdom amid complexity.

We learned in Chapter Three that decision-making is affected by the sequence in which we receive information, and that we are primed to react based upon the initial data we receive. Accordingly, the leader who speaks often to assert their point of view has a direct effect on the manner in which we consider complexity. Unfortunately, such leaders propagate their own blind spots and in essence, they infect their colleagues with their points of view. For the quiet ones, we need a process that fits their style and safely amplifies their perspectives.

In order to expand the collective perspective, and not magnify the perspectives of only the talkative few, it's best at the beginning of the process to have each individual determine and write down their own perspective of reality—undisturbed by outside input. This opportunity to independently consider opinions yields more data and subsequently yields more wisdom while also guarding the team against envisioning a limited perspective anchored in the blind spots of the ones who spoke first, or the loudest.

Create Shared Reality

Historically, creating shared reality with colleagues who disagree among themselves, or with an organization's chief, has been a difficult proposition for even the most well-meaning leader, as few are ever taught how to bring colleagues together to make sense of complex issues. Understandably, you might pause and wonder, "What if my colleagues disagree?" "What do I do if someone tries to dominate the discussion?" "What do I do if someone refuses to talk?" "Should I share my thoughts?" It all seems so risky. Perhaps you never developed a process to accomplish such a task.

Throughout the rest of this and the next two chapters, you will learn specific tactics you can use to bring diverse and at times contentious perspectives together to develop a shared sense of reality about complex challenges. Your job as the leader during this process is to facilitate learning as you guide your colleagues through a formal process of decision-making. You will learn to set up an environment in which colleagues may listen, learn, and be heard. The process will protect you and your colleagues and inspire trust. Much as a playbook tells each player on a sports team where to go and what to do, a decision-making framework provides a map of what will occur as you move through the process. As individuals understand that they will be heard and that their opinions matter, they relax and allow others to also be heard, and many of the fears and worries about the process dissipate.

NOW WHAT?

To access slides, handouts, and scripts designed to help guide you through the facilitation process, please see the Resources section at the end of this book.

Capture Perspectives

There are three basic means by which you can capture the perspectives of your colleagues: electronically, through interviews, or in person as a group. The method you choose will depend on the time and resources available. For example, if you have time and your colleagues are local, have an in-person meeting; otherwise, electronic capture or individual interviews may be the best approach. If there are outside perspectives you want to capture, or you would like to preserve the anonymity of the perspective, a one-to-one interview may be the best method.

Method 1: Capture Perspectives Electronically

Step 1: Send a "What Are Your Perspectives?" worksheet to each colleague.

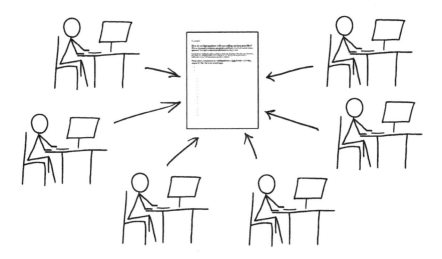

To capture perspectives electronically, send each of your colleagues the illuminating question (e.g., "How do we best combine our product development teams following the merger?") and ask them to write down their thoughts in bulleted form. You may choose to send them a document titled "What Are Your Perspectives?" The document could include prompts that ask about the strengths, weaknesses, opportunities, threats, fears, and worries associated with the illuminating question. (See the Resources section at the end of the book for information on where you may download a "What Are Your Perspectives?" template.)

What Are Your Perspectives?

[Insert The Illuminating Question Here Before Sending]

What are the strengths, weaknesses, opportunities, and threats related to our question? What are our fears and worries? How might we improve our effectiveness moving forward?

Please submit your perspectives in the bulleted form to [name] by [deadline: month, day of week, and date.] Feel free to use several pages.

-
-
-
-
-
-
-
-
-
-
-
-
-
-
-
-
-

Step 2: Each colleague sends the completed form back to you.

It is a best practice to assign a due date and to send reminders to your colleagues to reinforce the importance of their input and how much it is valued.

When the question is about a topic that is emotionally charged or when there is a low sense of psychological safety, ask that each respondent return the completed questionnaire to a trusted third party.

There is no place for the individual's name on the "What Are Your Perspectives?" document. The goal of this exercise is not to know who holds each perspective, but rather to make sure that perspectives are shared.

Step 3: Consolidate each of the bulleted responses onto a single shared reality document.

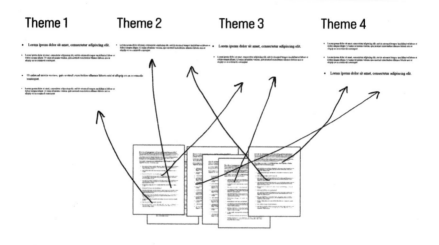

After you receive the completed form, write each bulleted entry from each document on a single shared reality document. Be sure to include the entries and themes you documented in Chapter Eight. As new themes emerge, add them to the evolving shared reality.

Edit out perspectives that negatively call out specific individuals or that fail to appreciate and respect differences of opinion.

Step 4: Present the shared reality to your workgroup.

Put together a slide presentation along with the master shared reality document you created, and present it to the group. During the presentation, which can be done either in person or during video conference, ask about what perspectives might still be missing. Finally, invite colleagues to either share additional perspectives during the presentation or to email them to you (or the trusted third party).

Method 2: Capture Perspectives through Individual Interviews

In some circumstances it may be most efficient to interview key individuals about their perspectives of the complex challenge. For example, a senior leader might be more responsive to answering your questions by phone or video conference, rather than by electronic form. There may be outside perspectives you want to capture. Time constraints may prevent certain individuals from attending a meeting or retreat. The interview provides an opportunity to capture their perspectives despite such obstacles.

When you interview a colleague, you can simply ask them about their perspectives of the strengths, weaknesses, opportunities, threats, fears, and worries associated with the illuminating question.

You may use the "What Are Your Perspectives?" worksheet as a prompt. You either write your colleague's responses down as you have the discussion, or you record their responses for transcription. After each conversation, transfer each bulleted perspective by theme into the summary shared reality document.

Finally, put together a slide presentation with the master shared reality document and share it with your colleagues.

Method 3: Capture Group Perspectives in Person

Step 1: Set ground rules.

As you start an in-person sharing process, it's a good practice to set ground rules for participation that encourage the development of positive group behaviors, and then to have the group agree upon them.

Here are the ground rules, before we start:

- Remember our core values of teamwork, respect, compassion, and integrity.
- Be curious, with a learning mindset.
- Appreciate and respect differences of opinion.
- Stay present and on topic.
- Maintain eye contact and actively listen when colleagues speak.
- Avoid side conversations.
- Be forgiving.
- Do not call out anyone negatively by name.
- Leave your title at the door. We're all colleagues and each of our opinions matters equally.

A show of hands, please. Do we all agree?

Step 2: Capture individual perspectives.

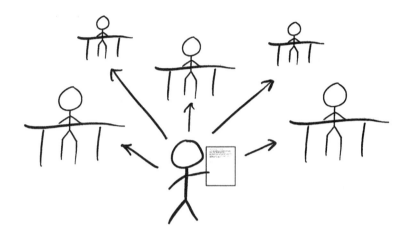

Give each colleague an opportunity to document their perspectives alone, before hearing what the others think. You can either ask each colleague to write their perspectives of the strengths, weaknesses, opportunities, and threats related to the illuminating question on a blank piece of paper, or you can distribute the "What Are Your Perspectives?" document to each of the meeting participants.

Then you might say, "Let's each take _____ minutes alone to quietly write down what we think about _____." You may vary the time depending on the total time of the meeting and the complexity of the topic being discussed.

Some individuals like to be physically alone while thinking independently. They may sit or stand in other parts of the room or even outside the room away from colleagues as they collect their thoughts; other individuals may be content to remain in their seat, next to their colleagues, but entering the individual opinion zone alone. Be prepared to offer options of thinking environments when circumstances permit.

Step 3: Assemble into small groups to share perspectives.

After the time allotted for individual thinking has ended, have your colleagues assemble into small groups to share their individual perspectives. Generally, it's wise to target three to seven people for each small group. Let the participants assemble into groups by themselves, unless you need to form specific groups to optimize psychological safety. This is discussed further below.

Set a time limit for group sharing: "You have the next forty-five minutes to share your perspectives." Supply whiteboards or poster boards for the group to capture their shared perspectives and assemble them into themes. Each group should select a scribe: "Please select a scribe to legibly keep track of each of the perspectives. You may write each perspective directly on the [poster board] or you can write each perspective on a different sticky note." The scribe can also help ensure that ground rules are followed.

There will be times when colleagues have opposite perspectives:

Director of sales: "It's the responsibility of the marketing team to discuss this feature with the client."

Director of marketing: "The sales team needs to discuss this feature with the client."

Program manager: "It is unclear who is supposed to reach out to the client."

Reinforce to your colleagues that differences in perspectives are expected and that there is no need to attempt to prove or disprove one statement over the other. Simply share and write down each perspective. The team will have an opportunity to reconcile conflicting perspectives later in the process.

To help facilitate the generation of themes, reserve time near the end of the process to identify them: "You have twenty minutes left. Start to group your ideas into themes." The use of sticky notes makes it easier to move perspectives around as themes emerge.

Step 4: Group presentations.

After small group sharing time is up, have each group present their key findings to the other groups. As each group presents, ask that subsequent groups share perspectives that have not been shared by previous groups.

NOW WHAT?

Which complex issue can you discuss today for thirty minutes with your executive team?

- Before you move to options and action, take fifteen minutes to privately write down your perspectives about the issue.
- Then take fifteen minutes and share perspectives.

Schedule a four-hour retreat with your board, executive committee, or workgroup to create shared reality around a complex issue.

- Meet with your leadership triad to identify potential obstacles that you may encounter as you facilitate the discussion.
- Identify whether you will have teams use sticky notes or whiteboards or large pieces of paper to capture each perspective.

Schedule the meeting, the location, and plan for any additional supplies you will need.

When small group sharing has been completed, save the entries by either taking pictures of each whiteboard or grab the poster boards. Then, if time permits, you (or your administrative team) can assemble each of the small groups' perspectives into a master shared reality document to be shared with the entire group.

As you move through the process of creating your shared reality, you may want to consider the following additional tactics.

Encourage Everyone to Stay in the Shared Reality

During the process of sharing realities, someone may jump ahead and outline an option for moving forward. For instance, a person might say, "We need to create a combined marketing and sales team to reach out to the client" before the creation of shared reality is complete. This makes sense. As people hear different perspectives, they gain insight and may reflexively process their intuitions out loud.

Gently steer discussion about "what we might do" back to discussion of shared reality. "That's a great idea. Let's save that for when we consider our options. For now, let's concentrate on understanding what people are sensing in this moment about [our issue]." Prematurely moving to "what we might do" before completing the construction of shared reality undermines an opportunity to share ideas, look around blind spots, and respond to complexity.

Group Individuals by Level of Power and Authority

Depending on the dynamics of the group, you may need to assign individuals with similar levels of power to their own tables. Otherwise, people with less authority in the organization may feel at risk if they share perspectives. For example, during a recent research lab retreat we divided tables into senior scientists, post-doctorate researchers, students, and laboratory technicians. If we hadn't divided the groups, there would be a risk that the students, for example, might have felt uncomfortable discussing their points of view in front of the senior scientists who grade them. However, when the students are together at a single table, they are empowered to share their thoughts with each other as they remain anonymous to those outside of the group. Then when the different groups share, one of the students acts as the spokesperson to discuss their shared reality. This not only decreases the perceived risk for the students, but also decreases the chance that a scientist would feel that they are being singled out by one of their students.

If you're in an organization in which confidentiality is a serious concern, you may want to engage an outside professional to conduct and collate the interviews. That way, you help the participants feel at ease sharing their thoughts.

Bring Forward the Elephant in the Room

Imagine a situation in which people are afraid to say something out loud. They are afraid to discuss the elephant in the room. They will not share their thoughts if they think others will be able to identify the source. They don't want, for example, a powerful board member, who knows the state's governor and virtually controls the local real estate market, to identify them as the source of the comment.

One option is to have individuals write their thoughts on sticky notes or notecards and hand the notes to a trusted scribe, who then reads and writes each comment on a whiteboard. Without that safeguard, others may recognize someone's writing or be aware that a certain person used a red pen. Having a scribe write out each comment preserves each person's anonymity. The best scribe in these cases is either a highly trusted individual from within the group or a trusted individual brought in from outside of the group.

Another option in this situation is to interview individuals so that contentious issues can be brought forward anonymously.

Broaden Your Perspectives

Who else's perspectives would increase the accuracy of your shared reality? Which individuals' or organizations' viewpoints have you missed? When you leave out crucial perspectives, you limit the effectiveness of the actions you will take later in the ROW Forward process. Perhaps you will choose to interview one or two others— individuals outside of your usual sphere of influence—to strengthen the diversity and accuracy of the perspectives within the shared reality.

NOW WHAT?

Hire a professional coach or facilitator to perform qualitative interviews about a contentious complex issue.

- Have them collect the anonymous input of your colleagues and place them into themes.
- Then schedule a meeting to discuss the collected shared reality.

What's Next?

In this chapter you've learned how to bring the diverse perspectives of your colleagues together to document shared reality. In the next two chapters we will build upon the shared reality that you and your colleagues have created to ensure that you incorporate the fears and worries of colleagues as you progress toward creating a shared vision for the future.

Executive Summary

➤ Wisdom is the ability to consider different perspectives.

➤ Wise teams and organizations promote diversity of opinion, nurture the independent generation of ideas, seek the viewpoints of both internal and external experts, and create shared reality before moving to action in complex scenarios.

➤ Diverse teams generate greater financial return, innovation, fact-finding, objectivity, and decision-making than do teams that lack diversity.

➤ To facilitate diversity of opinion, create teams with diversity in mind, bring in different personality traits, welcome disagreement, measure diversity, and seek divergent perspectives.

➤ To facilitate the development of independent opinions, encourage colleagues to step up to the balcony alone before sharing their thinking with others; optimize the thinking environment; and use various tools to capture ideas.

➤ There are three basic approaches you can take to create shared reality. You may capture your colleagues' perspectives electronically, through interviews, or in person as a group. The method you choose will depend on the time and resources available and the preferences of those involved.

➤ To capture perspectives electronically, send each of your colleagues the illuminating question (e.g., "How do we best combine our product development teams following the merger?") and ask them to write down their thoughts in bulleted form. You may choose to send a document titled "What Are Your Perspectives?" to each person.

➤ In some circumstances, it may be most efficient to interview key individuals about their perspectives on the complex challenge.

➤ Create a slide presentation along with the master shared reality document, and share the captured perspectives with colleagues.

➤ To capture the perspectives of a workgroup while meeting in person, first set ground rules that promote sharing. Then capture individual perspectives and break colleagues into workgroups to share those perspectives. Each group can assign a trusted scribe to document their perspectives. When that is done, specify an amount of time for each group to identify their themes of discussion, followed by a presentation of each group's shared reality to other groups.

➤ Avoid moving to "what we might do" before completing the construction of shared reality, as doing so may undermine an opportunity to share ideas, look around blind spots, and respond to complexity.

➤ If you're in an organization in which confidentiality is a serious concern, you may want to engage an outside professional to conduct and collate the interviews into shared reality.

➤ Interview individuals outside of your sphere of influence to strengthen the diversity and accuracy of perspectives within the shared reality.

10

IDENTIFY FEARS AND WORRIES

ROW Forward Framework

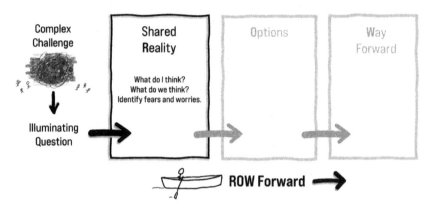

Fear lurks deep within our minds. We worry about what might occur if things change. We speak of action, yet our subconscious thoughts sabotage the very goals we champion. This happens to each of us individually, and it happens within our teams and organizations. We formulate well-intended goals. We detail plans. And then we get in our own way.

In this chapter, you will learn to uncover the fears and worries associated with complex challenges. When you surface the hidden commitments and the assumptions that arise from your worries and fears, you increase your likelihood of achieving difficult professional and organizational goals. As you acknowledge and name worries and fears, you bring them into the light of shared reality and you can challenge them.

Beowulf

The story of Beowulf is an outstanding business case study.[1] It is an epic poem written in Old English by an unknown author more than one thousand years ago.

Hrothgar, King of Denmark, is plagued by a lake creature named Grendel. During the day, the kingdom is filled with joyful feasts and gift exchanges. But by night, Grendel—the monster—rises out of the depths and tears people limb from limb.

There's a ready metaphor in the story. By day, leaders may go about their business feeling all is well. By night, their "monsters" rise up in their consciousness.[2] Their fears and worries threaten and terrify and ultimately, undermine their efforts.

The king hires Beowulf to defeat the monster, Grendel. Which (spoiler alert) he does. But after everyone has celebrated his victory and they all go off to bed, another monster emerges from the depths and goes on a rampage.

Despite an apparent victory, monsters still lurk.

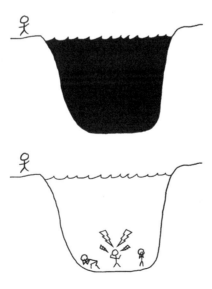

The Monster in Your Head

Jerry Colonna, my first executive coach and a coach for many startup CEOs, works extensively in the fears and worries space.[3] He calls our fears and worries "the monsters in our head."[4] He cautions us to recognize that the concrete challenges of day-to-day life are often not the cause of our suffering; rather, our suffering arises from the limiting beliefs born from the monsters in our own head.

A leader may speak about professional rivals or sales trends, but oftentimes they aren't really thwarted by those concrete challenges. Instead, what holds them back is the monster in their heads—the fear that doesn't turn up in most conversations but lurks deep within the recesses of their own consciousness. It's the fear that undermines their actions. It's the rumination that won't let them sleep at night. It's the unspoken reason they're not moving ahead with a strategy. To promote effective decision-making, a leader must not only confront their own monsters, but they must also help their team confront the monsters in their heads.

Immunity to Change

Robert Kegan and Lisa Laskow Lahey, developmental psychologists at the Harvard Graduate School of Education, designed a process to help leaders identify how fears and worries underlie limiting assumptions that prevent achievement of their goals. They call this internal goal blocking process Immunity to Change.[5] I use their framework frequently during both individual and team coaching and when facilitating change for large groups.

The Immunity to Change investigation begins after you identify a challenging goal. For example, consider one leader I coached who wanted to stop interrupting others during meetings.[6] Their goal was to "be better at knowing when to talk and when to listen." While they were very successful and highly intelligent, they knew that speaking out of turn was both a barrier to their continued success and a behavior that hurt those they lead. Despite knowing this and despite making repeated previous attempts to improve their behavior, they had not been able to achieve their goal.

The second step in the Immunity to Change process helps the leader identify the things they do—the specific behaviors they display—that work against achievement of their goals. While this leader wanted to be better at knowing when to talk and when to listen during meetings, they admitted that they still interrupted colleagues; had something to say about every item on the agenda; pressured colleagues to make uncomfortable decisions; and spoke loudly when they disagreed. When they tried to "just stop doing those things," the change would last for a few days, and then they would grow frustrated and fall back to their old ways.

Like the groundhog that gets frightened by its own shadow, the goal would retreat to the back of the leader's mind only to resurface at another time of dysfunction. After each failed attempt to improve, the leader would wonder, "What is wrong with me?" or "Is this just who I am?"

The third step of the Immunity to Change process—an ingenious step—challenges the leader to consider their worries and fears; the "monsters in their head" that prevent them from achieving their goal. They are asked to "imagine doing the opposite of each of those behaviors—the ones that that work against them achieving their goal—and then identify what discomforts, worries, and fears arise."[7] And in the process, as they express each fear and worry, they effectively name each "monster."

For example, as I coached the leader with the tendency to interrupt team members, I asked, "What would be your worry if you stopped interrupting colleagues?"

The leader responded, "That my point would be minimized and forgotten."

"What would be your fear if you didn't have something to say about every item on the agenda?"

"I would not be seen as a leader. A leader needs to know what to do in every situation, and showing uncertainty shows weakness."

"What would be the worst thing that would happen if you allowed people the time to consider their own opinions before pushing them to make a decision?"

"It would waste time. I already work too much and hardly see my family."

"What if, instead of speaking loudly with conviction, you spoke in a calm voice and admitted when you were unsure?"

"A leader needs to rally their colleagues to action. I worry that my colleagues would question my ability to lead and that I would become irrelevant."

During my coaching research, I have developed a sample list

of fears and worries I have heard from the leaders I have coached.[8] Leaders at all levels express the same concerns:

- I would lose control.
- I would lose my independence.
- I would feel constrained.
- I would be dependent on others.
- I would become expendable.
- I would not be liked.
- I would be alone.
- I would be seen as weak.
- I would be seen as vulnerable.
- I would anger or offend colleagues.
- I would be blamed.
- I would be seen as ineffective.
- I would not be respected.
- I would be unable to control my emotions.
- I am an impostor.
- I would not have enough time.
- I would not be myself.
- I would lose time with family or friends.
- I would not be heard.
- I would miss out on another opportunity.
- My presence would have no meaning.
- I would be seen as arrogant.
- I have risen above my capability.
- I am not a leader.
- I would be exposed as being incapable.
- I would be overwhelmed.
- I would not fulfill expectations.

- I would be unable to unite people.
- I would not be disciplined enough.
- I would break apart the team.
- I would lose power.
- I would be seen as disloyal.
- I would be disconnected.
- I would not grow.
- I would not be asked again.
- I would be uninspired.
- I would waste my time.
- I would not reach my ultimate goal.

NOW WHAT?

Which of the fears and worries listed above resonate with you?

How do these fears and worries surface in your decisions and your daily interactions with colleagues?

Behind each fear and worry lurks a subconscious commitment contrived to silence this leader's monsters. A commitment to not be minimized and forgotten. A commitment to not be seen as weak. A commitment to not waste time so that they might see their family. A commitment to not be seen as irrelevant.

And each commitment inhibited the change in behavior necessary to achieve their difficult goal. On the one hand, they wanted to be better at knowing when to talk and when to listen, but on the other hand, they didn't want to be minimized and forgotten, seen as weak and irrelevant, or not have time with their family. This bind created an immunity to change. The leader's subconscious thoughts—their fears, worries, and commitments—competed against and prevented them from achieving their goal.

It might be easy for you and for me to see the flaws in the assumptions that arise from such a leader's hidden commitments, such as the assumption that they need to speak loudly and interrupt others to prove their point, or risk being seen as weak and irrelevant. We understand that when a leader listens and admits that they don't know the answer, it often boosts the perception of a leader's abilities, rather than the opposite. We know that interrupting people and pushing them to make quick decisions can make colleagues feel exposed and result in worse outcomes.

The following are a few examples of limiting assumptions that leaders I have coached have held, and some brief comments to reframe each perspective:

If I don't micromanage, things go wrong.

It is important to hold oneself accountable to meet organizational goals. But, perhaps when this leader micromanages, their colleagues miss out on opportunities to learn essential skills. They inhibit their colleagues' professional development, and this hinders the organization's ability to scale and meet new demands. In fact, the leader's micromanagement may be a reason colleagues leave the organization and why it has been difficult attracting top talent.

If something bad happens, it's because of something I did or did not do.

Certainly, there are times when our actions result in unintended outcomes. But perhaps there are times when bad things happen in spite of a leader's actions. The world might evolve despite this leader's best intentions and actions.

I will lose the respect of my colleagues if they see I don't know what to do.

Perhaps the leader loses the respect of their colleagues when they act like they know what to do at all times.

I need to stay busy right now or I might, because of decreased productivity, be at risk of losing my job.

It is important to be a productive member of the organization. However, within a brief time frame, this leader had divorced a spouse and a parent died. Through the process of coaching, this leader created space and time—space and time that their colleagues, in fact, wanted them to take—for catharsis and to refocus. Their fear of losing their job if they took time to grieve and nurture their mental health grew from the monsters within their own thinking.

In order for me to be useful, others' priorities are more important than my own.

Or, perhaps when a leader makes others' priorities their own, they limit their ability to be their best self, and limit their colleagues' personal growth.

When I give difficult feedback I either crush or anger the individual, and as a result, I could lose a friend and colleague.

On the other hand, when feedback is given with empathy and a sincere interest in the personal and professional development of a colleague, it may strengthen the mutual working relationship.

If I don't push myself and say yes to things, then I will not grow.

If the leader continues to push themselves, they may continue to be overwhelmed, and they will not grow. Perhaps growth comes from a strategic combination of stress plus rest.

I can trust that a struggling individual will catch up by themselves, without my needing to create specific corrective actions. They should be able to take care of it themselves.

Or perhaps this leader's lack of direction and oversight reflects a lack of the leader's understanding in their own mind of how best to help colleagues develop professionally.

The leader often suspects that their monsters may not be real; they may know that their assumptions are flawed—and yet the monsters, with their tight grip of fears and worries, still reduce the leader's likelihood of success.

As a leader takes a deep dive into the waters of their subconscious thought and names the monsters that lie beneath, they shine light on dark, inhibiting perspectives. And quite commonly, through this process of discovery, their monsters disappear, and the leader achieves their goal.

The Fears and Worries of Organizations

Teams and organizations also possess unspoken fears and worries that prevent them from achieving goals.

I work with organizations that send their leaders to Mayo Clinic to take part in collaborative programs focused on improving employee well-being. Prior to the programs, each organization devotes considerable time and effort to working on well-being projects. Many have seen improvements, while others not so much. Each organization wants to improve employee well-being, but there are situations in which, despite investing time and effort, things don't change.

I help the leadership teams of these organizations discover whether or not they possess an immunity to change. During one program I asked a leadership team, "What are some things that your team does (or does not do) that prevents improvement of employee well-being?"

They responded, "We are not routinely measuring well-being. We are not getting input from people outside of our team. We prioritize other, more important issues. We are not getting feedback or asking for support from our CEO."

"What would be your worry if you started routinely measuring well-being and burnout in your organization?"

"That we would be blamed if well-being does not improve."

"What is your fear if you were to get input from individuals outside of your team?"

"That we would be overwhelmed with uninformed input."

"What's the worst thing that would happen to your team if you prioritized working on well-being?"

"We'd find that we cannot work on well-being and still put out the daily fires. Essential work would slip through the cracks."

"What would be the fear associated with seeking the feedback and support of the CEO?"

"That our CEO is too busy, and we would be seen as weak because we asked for help."

As you read through this list of responses, you may recognize similar concerns in your own team. Would any team want to be blamed for a lack of improvement, and be overwhelmed and unable to put out the daily fires, and find out that their boss sees them as weak?

This team assumed that there was not enough time in the day to perform essential work and also work on their challenging goal. They had not discussed how they might create time for their well-being work and still have time to put out fires. Nor had they discussed the amount of time that burnout squanders for an organization, with the resultant increase in employee turnover, decrease in quality of work, and diminished productivity.

They assumed that if they approached the CEO with their challenges, they would be seen as weak. The team hadn't approached the CEO and had no idea how the CEO would react, or what the CEO's thoughts would be about their relative strengths.

Assumptions like those may at times be accurate. Perhaps the CEO really is a vengeful monster ready to pounce—such behavior is well-known. The team could still deliberately discuss how to find the support needed for their project without jumping into the jaws of the demon. And perhaps the track record for receiving value-added input from individuals outside of the team is lacking. Still, there may be ways the team might incorporate input from colleagues in a way that is helpful, and not overwhelming. When teams discuss their fears and worries and identify potentially limiting assumptions before moving to action, they increase their chances of being effective.

When we examine this leadership team's fears and worries and hidden commitments and then look back at their goal of improving employee well-being, we can understand why their strategies fail. Their goal put one foot on the gas pedal, but their fears and hidden commitments put the other foot on the brake. They were stopping themselves from moving forward. They had created an Immunity to Change.

The fears and worries within our organizations, and our associated hidden commitments, are often unspoken, but they are reliable and reproducible drivers of behavior. We don't discuss them, but we obey them, even unwittingly.

Bring Your Fears and Worries into Shared Reality

All the good decisions in the world won't help you if you're afraid to follow through and act on them. Fear is not a story in your head or a creature beneath the waters. It is a real barrier to your best strategies. It is an obstacle that must be faced and fought.

In previous chapters you spent considerable time and effort documenting shared reality with your colleagues. Make sure that the fears and worries of your colleagues are embedded within shared reality. If they are not explicitly stated, you still have time to add them before you create shared vision.

NOW WHAT?

Ask, "What are the behaviors, the things our team does or does not do, that work against us achieving our goals?"

Then ask, "What are our fears and worries if we do the opposite of those limiting behaviors?"

Add your fears and worries to your shared reality.

What's Next?

In the next chapter, you will learn how to create shared vision from shared reality. As you develop shared vision, you and your colleagues will agree on whether or not to move forward with your complex challenge, you will ensure that your vision supports organizational mission and core values, and you will work to minimize the risks highlighted by the fears and worries that lurk within your team's shared reality.

Executive Summary

➤ Our fears and worries are the monsters in our head that prevent both individual and team attainment of organizational goals.

➤ The Immunity to Change framework developed by Robert Kegan and Lisa Laskow Lahey guides a process to help leaders identify the fears and worries and assumptions that prevent achievement of goals.

➤ By naming fears and worries, individuals may challenge the associated assumptions that inhibit goal attainment.

➤ There are times when the assumptions derived from fears and worries are limiting, and there are times when they are accurate.

➤ To promote effective decision-making, a leader must help their team discover and challenge fears and worries.

➤ Fears and worries need to be considered as elements of shared reality.

CREATE A SHARED VISION

ROW Forward Framework

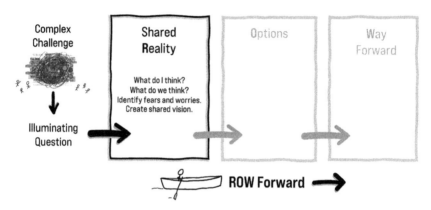

Some things just can't happen until the disco ball starts spinning.

We've considered getting off the dance floor and stepping up to the balcony as a metaphor for how to conceptualize the decision-making process. But now think for a moment about the disco ball, spinning high above the floor, casting its sparkling reflections on dancers below.

I was in middle school when I went to my first dance. Dances had a predictable starting process. I would arrive early, and all the lights would be on. All of the awkward young teenagers would mill about the hall in groups waiting for the festivities to begin. Some of us would stand on the sidelines, alone and unsure. The room was a study in hesitancy.

Then, as the clock struck 8 p.m., the main lights dimmed, and the disco ball lowered. The music came up by A Flock of Seagulls or Human League or some other synth band. The spotlight clicked on, and the disco ball began to spin, sending its images all over the room, gathering us all up in its energy. As the ball rotated, we cast our insecurities aside, stepped onto the floor, and began to dance. The disco ball and its wavering light brought us all together.

It's that experience of coalescence that we're going to discuss here—the group decision to get off the sidelines and begin dancing. In this chapter, we examine the process—and the importance—of creating shared vision. Shared vision is the final step in creating shared reality.

As your team decides to move toward action, you need a centrifugal force that brings everyone together—the wallflowers, the folks milling about in groups—and gets them all dancing to the same tune. At a dance, that's literally the disco ball. In organizations, it is the shared vision.

Shared vision is the first step in the decision-making process that moves a group toward action. It's the process by which you as a leader convene the minds to gather around a consensus on how to move forward. You move your colleagues from an analysis of the past, the present, and the imagined future toward the creation of specific plans.

Given all that has been discussed, all the varied perspectives of complexity embedded within shared reality, your team needs to decide: Does it make sense to move toward action? And if so, how do you move forward together?

In this chapter, we will discuss the three steps involved in creating a shared vision. First, you convert your illuminating question into a vision statement. Then, you amplify organizational mission and values within your vision statement. And finally, you address the fears and worries you want to mitigate as you move to action.

Create a Vision Statement

The first step in crafting a shared vision is to decide whether it still makes sense to work on the complex challenge. Given the various perspectives and themes embedded within the shared reality, and the differences of opinion regarding the strengths, weaknesses, opportunities, and threats related to the illuminating question you've been investigating, does it still make sense to move toward action?

Recall the complex challenge faced by the hospital executive team in the Introduction to this book. The executive team considered this question: "How might we work with the cardiology group to strengthen partnership and consider options that will be mutually beneficial?"

After having developed a shared reality—informed by multiple perspectives—the hospital CEO asked the team, "Given our shared reality, does it still make sense for us to work on strengthening our partnership with the cardiology group?"

It's entirely possible that given the shared reality, the executive team decides not to proceed. It may no longer make sense to focus their time and efforts toward strengthening their relationship with the cardiology group. They may have found during the development of shared reality that other dynamics were at play, the situation was evolving in ways that were not initially evident to the executive team, and a better tactic at this time would be to pause on this focus and work on an entirely different challenge. In fact, given the shared reality, they realize that had they prematurely moved to action, they might have created a major problem. They would have harmed relationships they had worked hard to establish with several other physician groups in the community.

That question—"Does it make sense to move forward?"—is an important one. Not only does the question give the team an opportunity to step back and consider how shared reality affects their initial instinct to move to action; by bringing colleagues together to make the decision about whether to move forward, a leader increases the likelihood of buy-in and engagement with a shared vision.

If, on the other hand, the team decides to move forward, the first step in crafting a vision statement is to convert the illuminating question into a statement.

"How might we work with the cardiology group to strengthen our partnership and consider options that will be mutually beneficial?" would become the following vision statement: "We will work with the cardiology group to strengthen our partnership and consider options that will be mutually beneficial."

Similarly, "How do we retain top talent and maintain healthy margins during challenging financial times?" would change to an affirmation: "We will retain top talent and maintain healthy margins during challenging financial times."

During the creation of your vision statement, you may also either narrow or broaden the focus. For example, "How do we bring the technology team and the marketing team together to establish a collaborative workflow?" might broaden to bring another essential workgroup into the vision statement: "We will bring the technology, marketing, *and sales* team together to establish a collaborative workflow." Or perhaps the marketing team is a bit of a mess, and the initial vision narrows to this: "We will bring the marketing team together to establish a collaborative workflow."

NOW WHAT?

What is the vision statement for your complex challenge?

Amplify Mission and Values

The next step in crafting a shared vision is to address and amplify behaviors that align with organizational mission and values.

Recall that in Chapter Five, we discussed the importance of the leader embodying and modeling core values. We learned that culture is a combination of values plus behavior. And we noted how easily an organization's mission and values can become disconnected from one another.

Now, having developed a vision statement, you must first test whether your vision aligns with the organizational mission and then highlight the values your team will embody as you proceed.

Align with Mission

If your mission is to "educate the children of the world" and your vision is to "teach the adults of the world," you may want to consider the apparent disconnect. You could ask, "In what way does our vision statement support the mission of our organization?"

When there is a mismatch between mission and vision, you need to adjust either the mission of the organization or the vision for how to proceed. Otherwise, the behaviors and the intentions of your team will grow increasingly misaligned.

Embody Values

Having tested and ensured alignment between mission and vision, your next step is to highlight the core values your team is to embody—to personify—as you collectively move toward deciding the actions you might take.

A study by Donald Sull, Stefano Turconi, and Charles Sull published in the *MIT Sloan Management Review* found that these are the top ten corporate values as derived from a sampling of 562 large corporations:[1]

1. Integrity (65 percent of the corporations in the sample)

2. Collaboration (53 percent)

3. Customer (48 percent)

4. Respect (35 percent)

5. Innovation (32 percent)

6. Accountability (29 percent)

7. Social responsibility (29 percent)

8. Excellence (22 percent)

9. Diversity (22 percent)

10. People (22 percent)

The following examples show how you might pair vision with values.

"We will bring the marketing team together to establish a collaborative workflow *in a way that highlights collaboration, respect, and innovation.*"

"We will retain top talent and maintain healthy margins during challenging financial times *while highlighting our core values of diversity, integrity, and the importance of our people.*"

"We will work with the cardiology group to strengthen our partnership and consider options that will be mutually beneficial. *We will approach our vision with a focus on our core values of excellence, integrity, and accountability.*"

NOW WHAT?

What are the mission and values of your organization? How might you infuse them into your shared vision?

What values, apart from those that are among your organization's core values, might you consider adding to your shared vision?

Mitigate Fears and Worries

During the final step in the development of shared vision, you should call out those specific fears and worries—the hidden monsters—discussed in the previous chapter, shine a light on them, and deliberately state your intention to address and mitigate them as you move to action.

Often, fears and worries correlate with the domains of psychological well-being discussed in Chapter Four. Your colleagues will want to ensure that the group's shared vision aligns with their sense of purpose, autonomy, personal growth, environmental mastery, positive relations with others, and self-acceptance. And when there are fears or worries about misalignment, those fears and worries need to be addressed.

For example, if the shared reality reveals a fear that individuals will lose their autonomy and a worry that the value each person brings to the team will be lost, that fear and that worry can be addressed in the shared vision:

"We will bring the marketing team together to establish a collaborative workflow in a way that *enhances a sense of both autonomy and teamwork, improves well-being, and recognizes the value that each of us brings.* We will approach our vision with a focus on our core values of accountability, integrity, and respect."

NOW WHAT?

Contemplate the shared reality of your team and reflect on the worries and fears you want to mitigate. Then, address ways in which you might avoid or lessen the influence of these perceived obstacles in your shared vision.

What is the shared vision for how you and your colleagues would like to move forward in response to the complex challenge?

Shared Vision of Quaker Oats

Let's reflect on how you might have applied the shared reality and shared vision process to the case of Quaker Oats, which we discussed in Chapter One. Recall that in 1983, the CEO of Quaker Oats overplayed his expertise to purchase Snapple—because he liked the way their beverages tasted. The acquisition resulted in a cratering of Snapple sales and a loss of $1.4 billion in revenue for Quaker Oats. The CEO's decision was made without an understanding of the complexity involved in integrating Snapple into the corporation, yielding disastrous results for Quaker Oats.

Imagine you are taken in a time machine to the Quaker Oats of 1983, and you are a senior executive. Yes, your clothes have big shoulder pads, and you likely listened to Olivia Newton-John while doing your morning aerobics. But you also decide to have a private discussion with the CEO. Suppose that, as a result of your conversation, he decided against reflexively purchasing Snapple and instead worked with his team on the ROW Forward framework to inform their decision-making.

Your team creates a shared reality around the following illuminating question: "How do we decide which beverage company we should acquire to extend revenue growth?"

Several important items surface during the discussion of shared reality:

- The potential acquisition needs to have a strong brand.
- Net profit margins need to be greater than 15 percent.
- The Gatorade acquisition was very successful.
- Snapple is a potential acquisition—and it tastes great.
- Other potential acquisitions have not been investigated.
- Snapple leverages a locally aligned distribution strategy that is different from Gatorade's current process.   ·
- Any product acquired would need to be aligned with our manufacturing process.

After a lively discussion, your team creates the following initial vision statement: "We will work to acquire a beverage company that extends revenue growth and inspires health, fitness, and energy among our patrons."[2]

You help the team address several perceived risks by adding the following sentence to the vision statement: "We will ensure that the acquisition yields net profit margins above 15 percent, leverages our distribution network, and aligns with our manufacturing process."

What's Next?

You have now concluded the construction of shared reality. You began the process of creating shared reality in Chapter Eight by clarifying your own thinking about a complex challenge. In Chapter Nine, you brought in the perspectives of colleagues.

In this chapter, you've brought your team together to contemplate a shared reality and to decide how your team will move forward. You moved from a discussion of the past and present toward a vision for the future. As you crafted a shared vision for how to proceed, you assured alignment with organizational mission, you highlighted key values, and you ensured that the fears and worries you identified in Chapter Ten were addressed and mitigated.

In the next chapter, you will leverage your team's shared vision with the many perspectives of shared reality as you brainstorm the different options you and your team may have as you proceed toward action.

Executive Summary

- ➤ Crafting a shared vision is the final step of developing a shared reality.
- ➤ Shared vision is a statement of consensus that describes how a group wishes to proceed within the setting of a complex problem.
- ➤ As a group moves from the contemplation of shared reality toward the development of shared vision, they envision the future.
- ➤ The vision statement transforms the question about the complex challenge into a statement of how you wish to proceed.
- ➤ After discussing shared reality, you may decide not to proceed any further with the complex challenge.
- ➤ Test that your vision statement aligns with your organizational mission.
- ➤ When your vision and your organizational mission are not in alignment, you need to restate either your vision or your mission.

➤ Shared vision highlights key organizational values that the leader and colleagues will embody as they move toward action.

➤ Identify fears and worries and deliberately decide that you will attempt to mitigate them in your shared vision.

12

GENERATE MULTIPLE OPTIONS

ROW Forward Framework

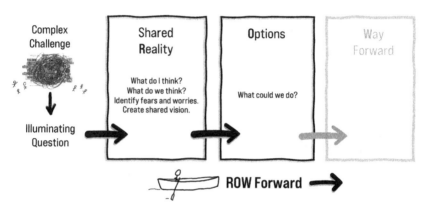

Now for the fun part.

After all the hard work of contemplating a shared reality and vision, it's finally time to formulate a specific plan for the future. This is the step in the ROW Forward process that feels most comfortable for most leaders. Now, rather than looking out from the balcony as an observer of perspectives, you start to actively point out how things may be changed.

The first objective in this chapter is to generate multiple options for what you might do moving forward. As you generate more options, you increase your likelihood of success. Then, after you create a long list of ideas for potential action, you whittle it down to identify the specific options you will pursue. Finally, at the end of this chapter you will learn how to overcome some of the challenges of group decision-making: What do you do when there is no consensus? What if someone strongly disagrees? Who makes the final decision—the team or the boss?

Generate Multiple Options

Remember Paul Nutt? He was the researcher from The Ohio State University[1] mentioned in Chapter Three, who noted that the likelihood of a successful decision increases when a leader involves others in the process. His paper, "Surprising But True: Half the Decisions in Organizations Fail," has a title that should make any leader shudder as they consider how they make decisions.[2] His research has shown that corporate leaders considered multiple options in only 29 percent of their decisions.[3] However, the success rate of decisions increased from 48 percent to 68 percent when multiple options were developed. The process of considering several options increased the likelihood of success and decreased the likelihood of failure.

Begin the process of generating multiple options by asking each colleague to privately reflect on this question: "Given our shared vision, what might we do moving forward?" Then have each colleague quietly write, in bullet form, every option that comes to mind.

This method mirrors the process used to generate independent perspectives within shared reality. The goal at this point is to create many different ideas for options. You do not want to get stuck in the blind spots of the persuasive few.

Next, have each team member share their ideas with the group. As each team member shares their ideas, their imagined option is written down for all to see. At this time, withhold opinions about the pros and cons of each new idea as it is presented. The primary goal at this point is to generate a long list of possibilities; the time for critical discussion will come later.

The specific process used to share ideas depends on the level of trust and the number of participants in the room. There are times when options may be shared in an open discussion or in small groups, and there are times when it is important to protect the anonymity of the individual generating each option idea. Refer to Chapter Nine for suggestions about protecting individual anonymity by using a combination of sticky notes and impartial scribes to record the ideas.

Examples of Options

Recall the hospital executive team's shared vision:

> "We will work with the cardiology group to strengthen our partnership and consider options that will be mutually beneficial. We will do so in a manner that fosters respect, integrity, and teamwork with a commitment to being stewards of community healthcare resources."

The hospital executive team wrote a long list of options that included the following entries:

- "Build a new cardiac catheterization lab."
- "Improve on-time start times of each procedure."
- "Perform procedures on weekends and evenings."
- "Develop our relationship with referring primary care physicians."
- "Learn about best practices from other hospitals."

Each new option revealed a different opportunity that the group might pursue.

Let's return to the story of Quaker Oats and its purchase of Snapple. The purchase was made based on the hunch of a single executive and the deal turned out to be a bad one for both companies.

How might it have played out if the Quaker Oats team had generated more options?

The executive team would move from considering a single option—"Purchase Snapple"—to considering multiple options developed during a brainstorming process:

- "Purchase Snapple."
- "Research other potential acquisitions."
- "Acquire a large beverage company with several holdings rather than a single brand."
- "Bottle and develop a brand of water."
- "Product line extension of one of our brands."

With this list of options, perhaps the company would have made a different, and less costly, decision. Sharing optional ideas often leads a group to think of even more concepts for potential options. Be sure to include these option add-ons as they arise.

The First Option

There is one option that is not written in either of the above examples. It is the first option for what anyone might do in response to a complex problem: Nothing. You may do nothing and attempt to retain the status quo.

Even though you agreed to move forward with a shared vision in Chapter Eleven, you still want to include that option of "Do nothing." Yes, even after all the work the group has done up to this point—weighing perspectives and envisioning; agreeing and disagreeing; uncovering the blind spots—there are probably individuals on your team who still think that things are fine just the way they are. And if you don't represent their inclinations on the list of options, their resistance will continue to surface from the darkness.

To borrow a saying used in coaching, "You don't have to change if you want to stay the same." Keep that in mind as you consider options. Write it down: "We can do nothing."

NOW WHAT?

What are the risks of doing nothing? What would it look like in the future if you attempt to retain the status quo?

Option Categories

Other than doing nothing, there are two other common option categories. The first category involves implementing a specific task, and the second category involves seeking additional information.

Implement a Specific Task

Examples of options that recommend the implementation of a specific task include:

- "Purchase Snapple."
- "Establish a workgroup to start a telemedicine program."
- "Create a process for marketing workflow."
- "Create an artificial intelligence workgroup."

Seek Additional Information

The following are examples of options that prompt further investigation of an open question, for which you will seek additional information:

- "Survey the beverage industry for potential acquisition targets that fulfill our criteria."

- "Conduct a ROW Forward with local distributors."
- "Research the best practices of highly effective marketing teams."
- "Examine the demand and capacity of our intake process."

Vanishing Options

There are times when we get stumped. We focus on what we reflexively want to do, and we have a difficult time considering any other ideas. In these situations, we only see one option: "We need to purchase Snapple or not." Or "the hospital needs to build a new cardiac catheterization lab or not."

The book *Decisive* by Chip and Dan Heath introduced me to a technique I use each day as I coach, and lead, and even as I make online purchases.[4] The Vanishing Options Test is a technique that prompts us to generate multiple options when we are reflexively stumped. The technique employs the services of a genie, but not what the book's authors call an Average Genie, which is the kind of genie that grants wishes. This process enlists the services of an Eccentric Genie—the genie that takes wishes away.

Average Genie asks the CEO, "What is your wish?"

The CEO responds, "I would like to acquire Snapple."

Average Genie grants the wish. And then Snapple sales crater, the distribution network revolts, and the CEO loses his job.

The Snapple example is a "be careful what you wish for" tale. I recall another one: a time when someone asked Average Genie for a million dollars. The wish was granted. And then one million dollars in coins fell from the sky and crushed the unlucky guy.

By contrast, the Eccentric Genie understands the nuances of complexity. Instead of granting wishes, Eccentric Genie eliminates them.

> The CEO asks Eccentric Genie to grant a wish: "I would like to acquire Snapple."

> Eccentric Genie responds, "You cannot. But what else could you do?"

> The CEO responds, "I would like to acquire a large beverage company that owns several leading brands."

> Eccentric Genie responds, "You cannot. But what else could you do?"

And as Eccentric Genie takes away each option, the list of potential options grows longer. When we get stuck, the elimination of a possibility prompts creativity.

There should be an Eccentric Genie available to illustrate the opportunity cost for every purchase.

> I say to Eccentric Genie, "I would like to click this button to purchase this large kitchen gadget I just read about for the first time to do this thing I have never done."

> Eccentric Genie responds, "You cannot. But what else could you do?"

> My response, "I could save for my daughters' college tuition. I could first learn to cook without the gadget. I could read a different article and find something else I definitely need to have."

I adapt Eccentric Genie's technique and make it a bit more practical when I help leaders generate multiple options.

The CEO tells me, "I would like to acquire Snapple."

My response, "That is a great idea. But let's just imagine that you couldn't do that. What else might you do instead?"

The CEO responds, "I would like to acquire a large beverage company that owns several leading brands."

Eccentric Genie responds, "That is also a great idea. But let's just imagine that you couldn't do that. What else might you do instead?"

When your team shares ideas, tell them the story of Eccentric Genie and respond to each idea by writing it down on the list of potential options. Then say, "That is a great idea. But let's just imagine that you couldn't do that. What else might you do?

> What if **you *couldn't*** do that?

NOW WHAT?

How might you apply the Vanishing Option Test in your daily decision-making?

Choose from Your Options

After you have generated a long list of ideas, it is time to explore the pros and cons of each prospective option. The following questions may help promote discussion:

- What is the benefit of this option?
- What are the downsides of this option?
- What are the limitations of this option?
- What other option(s) might be better?

After discussing each option, the group needs to select the specific option(s) you will pursue. A common approach I use is to have each individual pick their top three favorite options and submit them as a vote. Then, after the votes are tallied, it becomes clear which of the options has the most support. A subsequent discussion and/or vote may whittle down the list of options even further to arrive at the final option(s) the group will turn into action. Initially, it makes sense to have a smaller list of final options, perhaps choosing three to five options that the group will pursue. A larger list risks generating unneeded complexity as the group tries to move into action.

Challenging Situations

No matter how well the decision-making process is going, you're likely to run into a challenging situation along the way. Let's look at some common ones and ways to address them:

This Will Never Work

Remember the pessimistic character named Glum from Chapter

Four? He would exclaim, "This will never work!"[5] His colleagues would say with a smile, "Be positive, Glum." And Glum would respond, "I'm positive this will never work."

It is quite likely that you work with individuals like Glum. And when they say that something "will never work," you need to put your own emotions aside to examine whether there is opportunity in the pessimism. Perhaps there is a risk that could be called out and mitigated in the statement of shared vision. Perhaps more information and an expansion of your shared reality is needed. Or, perhaps Glum is pessimistic by nature no matter the circumstance. You may acknowledge Glum's concerns by repeating them back to the group or writing them down to memorialize those reservations for all to consider, and then move on. Learn from Glum, but don't focus on Glum.

The Silent Majority

A more difficult variation of Glum's "This will never work!" occurs when a leader represents themselves as speaking for many others, who are "all against this option."

When, for example, the head of the organization's engineering team exclaims, "The engineers will never agree to this!" it is quite likely that the individual is not truly representing the informed perspectives of the silent majority of "all of the engineers." The engineers may either work from a limited impression of the complex situation based on the filtered perspectives and fears of their leader, or they may be completely unaware that they supposedly disagree with the proposed action.

When the silent majority is invoked, it signals an opportunity to directly engage with the group in question. You want to represent their sense of shared reality, which makes their individual input essential. The expanded shared reality will help the executive team identify better options moving forward and can counterbalance a powerful single voice of fear.

The Resistance

When choosing options to pursue, focus on those who are aligned, rather than the resistance.

Some individuals, teams, and organizations are already behind your shared vision. They want things to work, and they see the potential of the new direction. They are your early adopters, your aligned first followers.[6] Others, on the other hand, are not so sure, are uncomfortable, or perhaps are adamantly opposed. They are the teams of individuals named Glum led by a leader who invokes the silent majority. They are the resistance.

Let's suppose, for example, that the technology team at the north campus are opposed, but the technologists at the south campus are all for it. Work with the south campus team first, optimize the chance for success with the proposed option, and produce an early win.

You will face resistance as you lead. Do not focus on the resistance; you are unlikely to change the minds of the resistance early on. Learn from the resistance, but focus on the aligned first followers.

Focus on the aligned

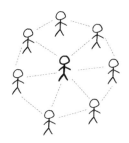

Not the **resistance**

The Tie Vote

There is a joke among physician leaders: "What do you call a 9 to 1 vote of yes versus no in a physician group?" The answer: "You call it a tie vote."[7] Because once the group hears that someone has voted no, everyone stops what they are doing, they cancel the results of the vote, and start the discussion all over again—perhaps meaning that a resolution cannot be reached.

In complex environments, do not expect a unanimous vote about the way to move forward. In fact, if the vote is unanimous, the situation may be complicated rather than complex. Thus, the vote on which options to pursue may be quite close.

When there are situations with significant disagreement you may want to choose options that seek additional information, rather than specific tasks for action. Then you can bring the results of the investigation back to the group for reflection.

On the other hand, there are times when action must be taken despite significant disagreement. The leader needs to step up and make uncomfortable, yet informed, decisions based upon shared vision. During such situations, it may be best to favor small experiments of action. We will discuss this further in the next chapter.

The Leader Decides

It is important to point out that the final choice of which options to pursue depends entirely on the culture of the organization.

Some organizations are highly collaborative in their decision-making process, and in these cases the team decides. There are times when the decision involves a smaller team—for example, an executive committee—and there are times when the decision-making involves a larger team of individuals, such as a whole department. In other organizations, a single leader makes the final decision. Whatever the case, in both circumstances the ROW Forward process informs the decision-maker about a complex challenge, and the broadened perspective of shared reality improves the likelihood of success.

NOW WHAT?

What challenging situations might you predict you will face as you move toward decision-making? How might you defuse the situation before it arises?

How difficult would it be for you if you needed to cast the deciding vote?

What's Next?

In the final chapter, each of the options you have chosen to pursue becomes an objective to be accomplished. You'll identify key members of teams, appoint individuals who are specifically responsible for each task, identify key results for each objective, determine timelines, and decide how you will show progress. And finally, as you move forward with each objective, you attain new knowledge and perspectives—data—that help you adapt to the complex world. You feed this data back into shared reality and ROW Forward to create new objectives that will increase your likelihood of success as you navigate the complex environment.

Executive Summary

➤ Generate multiple options for action to increase your likelihood of success in decision-making.

➤ Initially, individuals privately consider options for what actions might be taken moving forward. Then, individuals share their ideas to generate a long list of potential options for their team to contemplate.

➤ There are three categories of options: do nothing and maintain the status quo, implement a specific task, and seek additional information.

➤ Use the Vanishing Options Test as a technique to generate multiple options. With this technique, you imagine subtracting potential options as they appear. This promotes the creation of other ideas for options.

➤ Discuss the pros and cons of each of the options and then choose the options the group will pursue. One approach for choosing options involves having each colleague choose their top three choices and then deciding from the smaller remaining list of options.

➤ Challenging situations may signal a need for further investigation of shared reality, an understanding that a unanimous decision is unlikely, and an acknowledgment of the ways that fear surfaces during decision-making.

➤ Final decisions may be made either by the team or by the leader.

CHAMPION THE WAY FORWARD

ROW Forward Framework

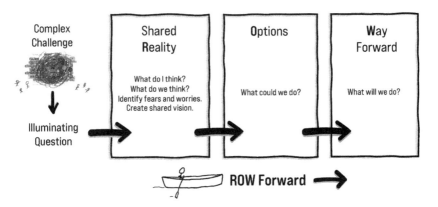

Perhaps the most dangerous moment of any decision-making process happens when everyone involved walks out of the room and heads back to their regular lives.

That's the point at which the decision—the thing you just spent time, resources, and brain power to craft—is most at risk. That's the moment at which your hard-won creation faces the cold reality of the outside world.

Will the decision survive?

We've all seen this happen. A group works hard to come up with a great idea and even a plan to execute it. But when the meeting breaks up, the magic may evaporate. The decision simply fades into the background of everyday life, and events may not move forward to realize what had been the potential of the decision.

This is the reason that the ROW Forward method has the word "forward" in it. It's the part of the decision-making process that often gets missed. It's not enough to come to a great decision. Leaders need a framework to take that decision and support its emergence into action. The idea needs to move forward.

In this chapter, we'll lay out how leaders can ensure that the "forward" part of decision-making does not get left behind. These critical steps will help ensure that your newly minted decision moves ahead.

Objectives and Key Results

Objectives and key results (OKRs) are the collaborative goal-setting framework of choice for many of Silicon Valley's most prominent companies. The original concept for OKRs came from Andy Grove, the former CEO and chairman of Intel Corporation.[1] John Doerr, a prominent venture capitalist and a student of one of Grove's management sciences seminars, evangelized OKRs to Google's founders. The methodology became an essential part of Google's management process, and spread to other technology companies in the Bay Area.

Each option you chose to pursue in the previous step of ROW Forward becomes an objective to be attained. For example, if you chose to pursue "increase telemedicine utilization," then one of your objectives will be to "increase telemedicine utilization."

Chosen Option ⟶ Objective

Each objective represents something you will do moving forward.

Additionally, for each objective, you need to define key results that describe how to know you have met that objective. How would you know if you have increased telemedicine utilization? One key result might be converting 10 percent of follow-ups from in-person visits to telemedicine.

Objective: What we will do?
Key Results: How will we know we've met our objective?

Key results may be framed as either a metric or a milestone. Generally, each objective has three to five associated key results.

Metrics   ## Milestones

   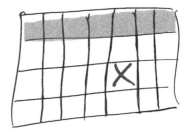

Metrics

Metrics define a specific quantitative outcome for your objective. They increase or reduce, they grow or eliminate, they build or maintain, etc. and they identify a specific numerical outcome.

For example:

- Increase revenue by 15 percent.
- Form a machine learning workgroup with five to seven founding members.
- Establish at least three initial OKRs for the machine learning workgroup.

Milestones

Milestones define a specific binary outcome—something you will do or not do. They may commonly be used for those objectives that involve seeking additional information. For example:

- Apply systems upgrade.
- Conduct a ROW Forward with the sales group.
- Establish the baseline capacity of the intake process.

Each objective may have several associated key results.

Objective: Improve utility of company intranet.
Key Results:

- Implement improved search engine.
- Improve design and layout of home page.
- Decrease home-page loading time by 20 percent.
- Increase home-page engagement by 35 percent.

Objective: Improve the recognition of each colleague's achievements.
Key Results:

- Create a weekly newsletter that identifies the important accomplishments of colleagues.
- Highlight important accomplishments at monthly department meetings.
- Recognize a specific accomplishment of each colleague at least once every quarter in the weekly newsletter.

- Improve the recognition score on the Leadership Behavior Index by 25 percent.

Objective: Decrease travel expenses by 35 percent.
Key Results:

- Implement new travel expense logging software.
- Establish the range of travel expenses by category for each workgroup.
- Audit the travel expenses of each colleague whose travel expenses per trip are > 1.5 standard deviations above the mean for each workgroup.
- Identify the top three travel expenses to reduce.
- Publish a quarterly travel tips newsletter.

Each key result within an objective should have a directly responsible individual (DRI) assigned to nurture and protect it and a specific date by which the key result should be completed.

Each objective team (OT) should report their results and findings to the leaders overseeing the ROW Forward process at regular intervals (for example, monthly).

To achieve each key result, it's likely that tasks will need to be delegated by DRIs.

Appoint the Directly Responsible Individual (DRI)

I facilitate retreats for groups of leadership teams tasked to solve their organization's most complex challenges. During the retreats these teams get to know and learn from other teams, which have their own unique challenges. During one retreat, an energetic and intelligent group of leaders displayed a wonderful sense of camaraderie.

They were fun to be with, and quickly befriended teams from other organizations. They accomplished the imperative work of creating a shared reality and choosing options to move forward during the retreat. However, after the retreat ended, this leadership team went home and their decision fell apart.

When I checked in on them, I could see the evidence all around me. They were about to miss their own established deadline. Nothing had been done. Their work was scattered at best. I gathered them in a video conference to find out what was going wrong.

"Who is the directly responsible individual?" I asked.

I heard silence.

They all looked at each other, wondering who would speak first. There had been no one individual directly responsible for moving the task to completion. And while the decision occupied space in each of their minds, the task struggled to survive. Each of them enjoyed working together, and each of them wanted to complete the task. Yet every one of them got caught up in solving the emerging issues of each day, and the task kept getting pushed to another time. The desire to achieve results was there, but the follow-up actions were missing.

A decision requires an individual responsible for its movement from a well-thought concept to an action-based reality. When an objective is left alone, without a voice, that objective is in jeopardy. The objective needs a steward who will protect it, and nurture it, and help it grow. This team needed to appoint a directly responsible individual to move the decision forward.

Adam Lashinsky devoted paragraphs in his book *Inside Apple* to the concept of a directly responsible individual and the way it fostered innovation and excellence within the company.[2] Consider this excerpt: "Any effective meeting at Apple will have an action list," said a former employee. "Next to it will be the DRI." Each task is assigned a directly responsible individual.

The DRI is the person assigned to each designated objective and key result to make sure the group produces results; they oversee and serve the needs of each task. A DRI helps the team navigate all manner of common problems that crop up to delay or derail a good decision. If the decision faces a mechanical or engineering problem, the DRI can keep the team investigating solutions until one is found. A DRI cuts down on stress that team members feel about "Who's got the ball?" Rather than worry about what other teammates are doing, each member works with the DRI to focus on their own specific tasks. In a fast-paced organization, a DRI keeps a good idea from getting lost in the fray.

Don't confuse the act of appointing a DRI for each objective with appointing a "boss" for the members of the project team. The DRI is a caretaker or a champion for the actions needed to complete the task, and not necessarily a boss of people in the working group. Each individual on the objective team still has their primary manager— their "boss"—whether inside or outside of the project team.

Although every decision needs a directly responsible individual, appointing a DRI may be more fraught than one might imagine. In today's business culture, with a focus on collaboration and teamwork, the process of appointing a leader of anything may at times seem counterintuitive. When we examine the potential stumbling blocks for self-managing organizations and matrix organizations, we see how decisions might get lost when there is no directly responsible individual.

DRIs in Matrix Organizations

In matrix organizations an individual may report to several managers.[3] For example, an engineer may report to their primary manager in technology, but also report to another manager in marketing for their work on a specific product. The role of the primary manager is essential to ensure that each of their direct reports has the time and resources needed to accomplish their work throughout the matrix. The primary manager needs to work with their direct report and the directly responsible individual to coordinate the most effective use of the direct report's time and resources. An engineer cannot, for example, devote 60 percent of their time to a technology project overseen by their primary manager and be expected to devote another 60 percent of their time to a cross-functional marketing project overseen by the marketing manager.

DRIs in Self-Managing Organizations

Self-managed organizations avoid what they see as the rigid top-down management structures of traditional organizational hierarchy.[4] They evade the formalities of leadership charts and rely on the dynamic formation of teams to accomplish work. Self-managed teams adapt their design and govern themselves to encourage flexibility and innovation.

Leadership responsibilities and task assignments within self-managed teams change depending on the needs of the work. But self-managed workgroups need to ensure that someone is responsible for each assignment. While individuals may be accountable for their specific tasks, someone needs to act as the directly responsible individual. The DRI "owns" the project to ensure that the workgroup goal is met and that the project remains relevant to higher-level organizational goals. When there is no directly responsible individual, the task may languish.

The first step for any team is to decide on a DRI for each objective—even if that seems to grate against the concept of collaboration and teamwork. There's nothing worse than making a great plan only to find that nothing gets done and everyone's time has been wasted. A DRI helps prevent that unfortunate outcome.

NOW WHAT?

Who will be the directly responsible individual for each objective and key result?

Choose the Objective Team

Now that you have assigned the directly responsible individual for the objective, you need to name the members of each objective team (OT). Each OT is to move forward on one of the options you choose to pursue. This ensures that each objective has both the directly responsible individual and the colleagues needed to achieve results.

Objective teams may include anyone. Some colleagues may have been involved throughout the ROW Forward decision-making process, while others are involved only in the implementation of objectives. Should a customer voice be included on the team? What about legal? Or a union rep? Assemble the team that can accomplish the goals.

How can you decide who to add to the objective team? Consider these questions:

- Who does the DRI need to work with to get things done?
- What does each member of the current team bring to the task?
- Where are the gaps in the team's approach?

An OT is best kept small—from two to five individuals. Otherwise, it's more like a loose committee than a team. When the OT grows large, things like scheduling conflicts become an issue. People go out of town, they have other responsibilities, they sit on multiple other committees, or they simply lose focus. Colleagues on a small team will be more accountable to one another. They can call on one another for help in a pinch. They will be less likely to shrug and assume that someone else will pick up the slack.

Each member of the objective team may operate on their own, or they may lead teams of other individuals to accomplish specific tasks within each objective. For example, the salesperson on the OT may work with larger teams of salespeople and account managers to work on a specific part of the task. And then as each task is accomplished, or roadblocks are faced, these team leaders bring their findings back to the OT for discussion. When objective teams work in this manner, they minimize the frequent "just keeping everyone in the loop" messages that plague the inboxes of team members in inefficient organizations. When OTs operate efficiently, they reduce the need for time-consuming all-hands-on-deck meetings. Essential individuals meet as needed to address the specific demands of the project. The objective team surveys the needs of the task and stays responsive and nimble.

Sometimes a ROW Forward is performed by a team of one (in other words, you). In such a case you may assign objectives and DRI responsibilities to others or you may decide to pursue the OKRs on your own.

Address Scheduling

Once your DRI and objective team are in place, you can get down to everyone's (least) favorite party game: scheduling. Technology such as online calendars can help in this effort, but however you make it happen, don't skip this step. Begin with the obvious question: When do we start? Ideally, that date is soon so that no momentum is squandered. But whatever date it is, commit it to writing. Then work out the details with colleagues:

- When, specifically, will you meet?
- How will you meet? Will it be in person? Via video conference? On a conference call? Via a messaging app? On a project management app?
- Who will schedule the meeting? Generally, the DRI is responsible for ensuring that meetings are scheduled and that the process keeps flowing. However, the subtext of this question is, who actually is in charge of each objective team member's schedule? Is each team member responsible for their own schedule, or do they have an administrative assistant who coordinates the schedule? There's no point contacting an objective team member if they're not the ones scheduling meetings.

Keep in mind the date on which the objective team needs to report back to the executive team about results and findings. Be sure to schedule enough time to show progress. Start the work as soon as possible.

It's quite possible, especially in smaller organizations, that the individuals on the executive team also act as the objective team for chosen tasks. When this is the case, be sure to not overextend and overwhelm each other. Be realistic about the amount of work that each of you shoulders. If it is possible, identify others who may take over responsibilities or pause other lower-priority projects and meetings. In those cases in which you have a team of only a few members, consider rotating the DRI for each task, rather than having the same DRI on each one.

When practical, objectives should be pursued in parallel rather than in sequence. The idea is to throw a bunch of objectives into the complex environment at once, rather than to pursue only one objective at a time, and then see what happens. For example, one objective team may work on a specific task, while another objective team investigates an open question, and a third team pursues a different objective.

Upon task completion (or at appropriate check-in intervals), each OT needs to present their results to the executive team. The objective team's findings provide the executive team both data and perspectives—which may be added to the evolving shared reality that the team considers as they plot next steps.

When possible, pursue objectives in parallel. Sequentially pursuing objectives "one-by-one" rather than in parallel needlessly prolongs the process. Your aim is to be nimble and responsive. Learn quickly and adapt to the ever-changing complex environment.

NOW WHAT?

How will you ensure that each member of the objective team has the bandwidth and the resources needed to complete the chosen option?

Delegation

As a team forms, errors of delegation are the most common cause of task failure.

When forming new teams, you may need to assign tasks to colleagues you've never worked with before. Do you know their level of experience? Do you agree upon what the task requires? How on-time will your colleagues be with their assignments? Unfortunately, you often don't know the answer to these questions.

Delegating is not always as easy as simply saying, "You do this!" When delegating a task you need to consider what you are specifically delegating and how well you know the competency of the individual assigned to each task. Assign tasks based upon your level of trust and familiarity with each colleague, and check in early to look for progress.

Consider the following three levels of delegation as you assign each task.

Level 1: Checkbox Delegation—"Do exactly this."

This is the simplest level of delegation. You assign a very specific task that you want completed in a specific way.

Examples:

- "Get the average salary for a database specialist from the U.S. Bureau of Labor Statistics for our metropolitan region as compared to New York City."
- "Meet with the housekeeping staff to get their input on what they perceive as the opportunities, weaknesses, and risks related to our current process."
- "Meet with our regulatory attorney to get their approval."

These tasks are like checkboxes on a to-do list. You set a specific date and see how well your colleague delivers results.

Level 2: Consider and Recommend Delegation—"Figure it out and bring me your recommendations."

These tasks require multiple steps and decision points. You give someone a topic. They gather the facts and consider the approach. Then they get back to you to discuss their findings and recommend the ways in which the team should proceed.

Examples:

- "Identify the software and hardware we should use to enhance remote work."

- "Figure out a process to ensure that we contact patients when there are critically abnormal laboratory values."
- "Consider the opportunity cost for a Snapple acquisition and give the team your recommendation."

While this is more advanced delegation, you remain an intrinsic part of the decision-making process. Your colleague filters through what is possible, figures out their approach, and you decide together.

Level 3: Complete Delegation—"This is your project."

Make someone the CEO of a project. You give them full responsibility and accountability. They make the decisions, they figure out the approach, and they get it done.

Examples:

- "I'm appointing you as the chair of our new telemedicine division. Build the team and get things started within budget."
- "We need you to organize our annual corporate retreat."
- "You are responsible for our southwestern territory."

This is the ultimate in delegation. You provide vision and clarify goals. You remain available as a resource and have occasional check-ins. But they own it.

When to Use Each Level of Delegation

The more familiarity and trust that you have with someone, the higher the level of delegation that you'll use with that person. When you first work with someone, it's more common to use level one or level two delegation. You check in frequently to protect and nurture the task and help your colleague. As questions arise, you have an opportunity to teach, learn, and when necessary, adjust.

Which To-Do to Delegate to Whom?

Step back and deliberately think about who should be responsible for each task. Be clear about which tasks you will complete and which tasks you will assign. A leader who views each team task as an item on their personal to-do list risks becoming overwhelmed, and also risks alienating team members. This may be a good time to review the fears and worries of the micromanager, which we discussed in Chapter Ten.

To-Do: A task that requires your completion.

Their-Do: A task you delegate to someone else to complete.

Our-Do: Tasks that require the presence of multiple colleagues to complete.

No-Do: The things you and your colleagues will say no to in order to accomplish priorities.

Do-Be-Do-Be-Do: The music that plays in your head when you deliberately and effectively delegate and assign tasks.[5]

NOW WHAT?

Who will you involve in the assigned work? When do they need to participate? How can you use their time most efficiently?

What level of delegation will you assign to each member working on each task?

The Way Forward

As you move forward to action, it is essential to think of each objective and key result as an experiment, to track the progress of each action, and to share the findings and results with colleagues.

Learn Fast and Fail Fast

Paul Nutt, the professor of management sciences from The Ohio State University mentioned in Chapter Three and Chapter Twelve, teaches us that even in optimal scenarios—using multiple perspectives to generate multiple options—decisions fail more than 30 percent of the time.[6] The goal is to fail fast and to assimilate what is learned. Each roadblock, each response, each added perspective provides data for the team to use to limit losses and create more effective objectives.

Think of each objective and key result as an experiment that layers the landscape of complexity. Each experiment pokes at the complexity. And with each nudge you get to see how the environment responds. The response may clarify or muddle. It may result in success, or it may result in failure, but it produces useful data either way.

Create a Tracking Board

Emergency departments use tracking boards to visualize which patients are in which room, what has been accomplished, what is pending, who is caring for them, and how long they have been there. The emergency physician and nurses can see it, other departments can see it, and when the tracking board is done well, each patient can see where they are in the process. How will your teams track progress?

A tracking board—on paper, spreadsheet, whiteboard, or in a project management database—shows all members of the objective and executive teams:

- The specific objective
- The directly responsible individual
- The members of the objective team
- The projected date for completion and the person who is the directly responsible individual for each key result
- When the next meeting will be
- When the objective team will report to the executive team
- The subtasks and who is responsible for each of them
- A summary field that briefly describes the actions/data/findings/work in progress.

The DRI may use the tracking board to run meetings and hold individuals accountable for each task. This keeps the team on track to nurture each task.

NOW WHAT?

When will you review the outcomes and the data of the initial ROW Forward process?

How will you use the data and experience added to the shared reality to generate other options?

Share Your Findings

Decide at this outset how you will share your findings. Will you share only with the leadership team of your organization? Will you include departments? Divisions? The full organization?

In Chapter Five we learned about eight leadership behaviors. Each behavior, when expressed by a direct supervisor, decreases the odds of burnout and increases the odds of professional satisfaction.

Colleagues want to be encouraged to suggest ideas for improvement, they want to develop their talent and skills, and they want to be kept informed about the changes taking place within the organization.

Involving people in the ROW Forward process encourages autonomy, alignment of purpose, personal growth, environmental mastery, and positive relations with colleagues—all elements of well-being.

Create a plan to communicate your progress and findings at meetings, through newsletters, and posters. Your team may be doing impactful work to improve the workplace and the effectiveness of your organization, but if you do not communicate your progress and your findings, most of your colleagues are unlikely to know that these positive developments are occurring.

NOW WHAT?

How will you communicate the findings of the ROW Forward process to celebrate your vision, values, and mission to other members of your organization?

ROW, ROW, ROW

The ROW Forward process is iterative. After the initial objectives have been completed, revisit and make sense of the resulting data. Some key goals may have been attained, while others remain unmet.

Perhaps an initial objective resulted in a dead end, whereas another revealed significant opportunity. Given these experiences and perspectives, your team now has an opportunity to add perspectives back into shared reality. Then consider new options for how to move to action. Each iteration of ROW Forward generates more data. Each new perspective derived from this data helps you understand the complex environment.

As you progress, your efforts may reveal domains of increasing clarity; some of the objectives your team pursues may reveal areas that are complicated, rather than complex, and you may enlist a group of experts to make decisions. At other times, a clear process will be discovered, and a new best practice formed. And through these iterations of discovery and action, what was once complex begins to morph into multiple components that are simply complicated, or even clear.

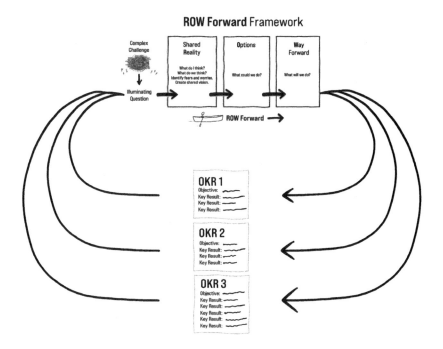

Case Study: The Boutique Hotel

Dalia, the CEO of the boutique hotel company from Chapter One, brought her executive group together during a retreat to formulate a near-term strategy for the hotelier. A tight labor market, the development of "green" practices, and changes in technology were shifting the hotel environment.[7] While the retreat went smoothly, the execution was bumpier than she had predicted.

The executive team chose to focus on three initial objectives.

Their first objective was to partner with local businesses and services within each region. To achieve this objective, they identified the following key results:

1. Provide four suggestions for high-impact partnerships within each region by the second quarter.

2. Establish service agreements with one new partner within each region by the third quarter.

Their second objective was to improve employee engagement and retention. To achieve this objective, they identified the following key results:

1. Train all leaders in ROW Forward and the Five Hats of Effective Leaders by the second quarter.

2. Create an "Our Stories" weekly newsletter by the second quarter.

3. Decrease employee burnout by 10 percent by year end.

4. Improve the Leadership Behavior Index by 20 percent by year end.

Their third objective was to enable real-time operations data for housekeepers. To achieve this objective, they identified the following key results:

1. Migrate data warehouse to the cloud by the second quarter.

2. Launch real-time housekeeping dashboard by the second quarter.

3. Train 100 percent of housekeepers to use the dashboard by the third quarter.

Each objective was assigned a directly responsible individual, and that individual set out to create the objective team and identify key results.

The first two objectives went smoothly. Key results were achieved, and findings shared throughout the organization. The information obtained during each project provided additional data and perspectives that would help the executive team consider next steps. The third objective, however, did not go as planned.

Dalia had appointed Steven, the chief technology officer (CTO), to serve as the DRI to work on enabling real-time housekeeping decisions. It quickly became evident that (a) Steven was underqualified for the task and (b) relationships between leadership and housekeeping were falling apart.

Steven was not meeting deadlines, and each meeting he ran left behind a wake of hurt feelings and confused colleagues. Dalia spent considerable time coaching Steven; however, he was not up to the task. Dalia replaced Steven with a more effective CTO.

Relationships with housekeeping were fractured during this process. Steven had not included key members of the housekeeping staff during several dashboard modeling discussions. Steven thought the discussions would be best handled by the engineers, as they were dashboard experts. This resulted in a dashboard that, while being technically sound, had poor usability for the housekeeping staff.

As a result, Dalia and her executive team identified improving the experience of housekeeping as a key objective. Dalia referred to the housekeeping staff as the heart and soul of the organization. While she assigned the vice president of operations as the DRI for the objective, Dalia was deliberate in meeting one-to-one with house-keeping staff during site visits to express her thanks and to check the pulse of the organization.

Executive Summary

➤ Each option you choose to pursue during the options step of ROW Forward becomes an objective with key results to be attained.

➤ Each objective represents something you will do moving forward. For each objective, you need to define key results that describe how you will know you have met the objective.

➤ Key results may be framed as either a metric or a milestone.

➤ Each objective has an assigned directly responsible individual. The DRI ensures the availability of resources, oversees the objective team, and navigates roadblocks to support task completion.

➤ Each objective has a team assigned to nurture and complete it.

➤ The size of the objective team is best kept small to ensure the efficiency and nimbleness of task completion. Other individuals or teams may be called in as needed to help the objective team complete tasks and subtasks.

➤ When practical, objectives should be pursued in parallel rather than in sequence. This creates the most experience and data from which to consider further options.

➤ Be specific about scheduling to maintain an efficient process and meet deadlines.

➤ Delegate tasks and subtasks to individuals using the appropriate level of delegation. Level one involves checkbox delegation, in which an individual is assigned to do a specific task in a specific manner. Level two asks individuals to consider a task and recommend actions. Level three delegation involves giving an individual full responsibility and accountability for designing and completing a task.

➤ Each objective and key result is an experiment. Some fail, and some are successful. The goal is to fail fast and to assimilate what is learned into the workflow.

➤ Use a tracking board to list the names of the DRI and team members for each objective; to track deadlines and completion of each objective and key result; and to communicate progress to other colleagues.

➤ The ROW Forward process is iterative. During each cycle of ROW Forward, new perspectives are created. Incorporate this data back into the shared reality to help the organization make sense of the complex world.

➤ Over time, complex challenges may reveal areas that are either complicated, requiring experts to reach decisions, or clear, in which case best practices may be applied.

14

NOW WHAT?

"As we grow in learning, we more justly appreciate our dependence upon each other. The sum total of [knowledge] is now so great and wide-spreading that it would be futile for [one] to attempt to acquire, or for any [one] to assume that [they have], even a good working knowledge of any large part of the whole. The very necessities [drive us] into cooperation. [A] union of forces is necessary."[2]

—Dr. William J. Mayo

In the pages of *You're the Leader. Now What?* you learned the frameworks and tactics of effective leaders. Will you translate what you have learned into practice? Or will you simply move on to the next leadership book, social media post, or article of the moment.

If you choose to approach leadership with a static mindset and lead as you always have, you risk putting both yourself and your organization at a disadvantage. Your best practices will become past practices, your effectiveness will wane.

Alternatively, if you embrace leadership as a profession of skill and wisdom—improved through hard work, reflection, and practice—over time you will become more effective.

Derek Sivers, a writer and musician, observes that ideas are worth nothing if not executed.[1] He asks us to imagine that a good idea is worth $10, and a brilliant idea worth $20. But even weak execution is worth $1,000, and great execution worth $1,000,000.

The value of standalone ideas is nearly nothing—about the cost of this book—when compared to the same ideas leveraged as multipliers of execution. Given this premise, a good idea multiplied by weak execution is worth $10,000, whereas the same idea accompanied by great execution is worth $10,000,000.

Before you close this book consider your ideas. How will you become a better leader? How will you put your ideas into practice?

Here are several actions for you to consider.

How will you lead one-to-one?
- Whom will you coach? When?
- Whom will you sponsor? How?
- How will you measure burnout and engagement?
- What specifically will you do to improve well-being and engagement?

How will you lead teams?
- What challenge will you and your colleagues choose to ROW Forward?
- How will you increase the diversity of perspectives on your team?
- What fears and worries need to be acknowledged and mitigated?
- How will you ensure that colleagues feel safe speaking up?

How will you lead yourself?
- What difficult professional goal will you pursue?
- When will you take time to reflect?
- What will you delegate to others?
- What limiting assumptions do you hold?

RESOURCES

Please contact me if there is anything I can do to help.

You can access and download slides, handouts, templates, and scripts designed to help you apply the leadership concepts within this book at: richardwinters.com/nowwhat

ACKNOWLEDGMENTS

To my family, thank you. I love you.

Thank you to the entire team who helped make this book. While I may not love you, I like you a lot. Thank you, Dan Harke, publisher of Mayo Clinic Press, for championing this book through the committees of committees. Nina Wiener, editor-in-chief; Rachel Haring Bartony; Jay Koski; and Kelly Hahn, thank you! Thank you, Philip Turner, John Landry, and Kate Petrella for your edits. Thank you, Ellen Neuborne for your help with the initial draft. David Wilk and Arthur Klebanoff, thank you. Thank you, Book Highlight and Fortier PR for your expertise during book launch. To my literary agent, Jim Levine, and to Courtney Paganelli, thank you. Thank you, Charlotte. Thank you, Bonnie!

Thanks to all the individuals mentioned in this book. You are my mentors from afar. Someday, you might invite me to tea. Then, as we sip our tea, we will laugh, and you'll tell me there is something in my teeth. I'll say, "Yes, I know. I put it there." And then we'll laugh a whole bunch more. And then we will wonder why we are laughing, so we will stop.

Thanks to everyone I have worked with now, in the past, and in the future. Your tolerance is appreciated. I know. I get it. I'm sorry. Let's blame the leader who hired me.

Thank you, Mayo Clinic, for living values and mission. Thank you to my colleagues in emergency medicine for meeting the needs of patients at any hour on any day. Thank you to my patients and their families for teaching me life.

Thank you for reading this book. Thank you for attending my talks and courses. Thank you for allowing me the privilege of coaching you. Thank you for putting in the hard work of developing yourself, your colleagues, and your organization. Thank you for leading.

ABOUT THE AUTHOR

Dr. Richard Winters is a practicing emergency physician at Mayo Clinic. As medical director of Professional Leadership Development for the Mayo Clinic Care Network, Dr. Winters delivers leadership development programs that train leaders at all levels of healthcare organizations worldwide. As a professional certified coach, Dr. Winters provides executive coaching for Mayo Clinic leaders.

Dr. Winters graduated from the Mayo Clinic Alix School of Medicine in 1994 and returned to Mayo Clinic in 2015. Prior to returning to Mayo Clinic, Dr. Winters served as managing partner of a democratic physician group, department chair of an emergency department, president of an 800-physician medical staff, and CEO/founder of a startup managed care organization that struggled to survive amidst the complex relationships among hospital, physician, patient, competitors, and insurance providers. He lives in Rochester, Minnesota, with his family.

ABOUT MAYO CLINIC

Mayo Clinic is consistently ranked among the top hospitals in the nation. Every year, more than a million people come to Mayo Clinic for care. Our highly specialized experts are more experienced in treating rare and complex conditions.

Successful treatment starts with an accurate diagnosis. Mayo Clinic doctors work together to find answers. They collaborate as team members. At Mayo Clinic, you don't get just one opinion — you get multiple opinions.

What might take months elsewhere can often be done in days at Mayo Clinic. We evaluate your condition from every angle to make the very best plan for you.

To request an appointment, go to: mayoclinic.org/appointments

NOTES

Introduction

1. **You're all incorrect. We will proceed with my plan.** I first heard this joke as told by Dr. Robert Hicks. Dr. Hicks was the founding director of the organizational behavior and executive coaching program in the Naveen Jindal School of Management at the University of Texas at Dallas. He is the professor who first taught me the science of executive and professional coaching.

2. Many of the names and stories in this book are composites of fiction and nonfiction. This is done to protect confidentiality and to illustrate educational concepts.

Chapter One: Recognize the Limits of Your Expertise

1. **Stumped.** Kahneman, D. (2011). *Thinking, fast and slow*. New York: Farrar, Strauss and Giroux.

2. **Leaders making reflexive decisions.** Paul Nutt's analysis of the acquisition of Snapple by the Quaker Oats Company. Nutt, P. C. (2004). "Expanding the Search for Alternatives during Strategic Decision-Making." *Academy of Management Perspectives* 18(4): 13–28.

3. **A great example.** I first learned of Paul Nutt's work when I read the book *Decisive* by Chip and Dan Heath. This book opened my eyes to the importance of process in decision-making. I strongly recommend that you read *Decisive*.

Heath, C. and D. Heath (2013). *Decisive: How to Make Better Choices in Life and Work*. New York: Currency.

4. Quaker Oats purchases Gatorade in 1983. Berg, E. N. "A Familiar Area for Quaker Oats." *New York Times,* July 21, 1983. https://www.nytimes.com/1983/07/21/business/a-familiar-area-for-quaker-oats.html. Accessed April 23, 2020.

5. A snap decision. Deighton, J. (2001). "How Snapple Got Its Juice Back." *Harvard Business Review* 80(1): 47.

6. Quaker CEO loses job. "$1.4 Billion Mistake Costs CEO His Job." Millman, N. *Chicago Tribune*, April 24, 1997. https://www.chicagotribune.com/news/ct-xpm-1997-04-24-9704240169-story.html. Accessed April 23, 2020.

7. What's more important, process or analysis? Heath, C. and Heath, D. (2013). *Decisive: How to Make Better Choices in Life and Work*. New York: Currency.

8. Process vs analysis. Lovallo, D. and Sibony, O. (2010). "The Case for Behavioral Strategy." *McKinsey Quarterly* 2(1): 30–43.

9. Dr. Trastek and Shelly Olson. Dr. Victor Trastek on Leadership Lessons Learned from a Nurse—Mayo Clinic. YouTube. March 3, 2014. https://www.youtube.com/watch?v=-SN5IzeO6kU. Accessed January 11, 2022.

Chapter Two: Map Your Decisions

1. The Cynefin Framework. Snowden, D. (2002). "Complex Acts of Knowing: Paradox and Descriptive Self-Awareness." *Journal of Knowledge Management* 6(2): 100–111.

2. The Cynefin Framework. Snowden, D. J. and Boone, M. E. (2007). "A Leader's Framework for Decision Making." *Harvard Business Review* 85(11): 68–76, 149.

3. The five domains of Cynefin. In the Harvard Business Review paper noted above, the five domains of the Cynefin framework were labeled as obvious, complicated, complex, chaotic, and disordered. Mr. Snowden has changed the domain names from obvious to clear and from disordered to confused. The Cognitive Edge website offers numerous blog posts and training opportunities to further understand the Cynefin framework. I encourage you to look further into his writings and consider enrolling in the programmatic offerings at Cognitive Edge. Snowden, D. J. (2020). "Cynefin St David's Day 2020 (1 of 5)." https://thecynefin.co/cynefin-st-davids-day-2020-cynefin-framework/. Accessed February 14, 2022.

4. **Testing criteria for sore throat.** The testing scenario in this chapter is based upon a patient's age of fifteen years to forty-four years. Harris, A. M., et al. (2016). "Appropriate Antibiotic Use for Acute Respiratory Tract Infection in Adults: Advice for High-value Care from the American College of Physicians and the Centers for Disease Control and Prevention." *Annals of Internal Medicine* 164(6): 425–434.

5. **Strep pharyngitis care management model.** Ask Mayo Expert: https://askmayoexpert.mayoclinic.org/topic/clinical-answers/cnt-20131920/cpm-20130331. Accessed October 3, 2020.

6. **Best practice is past practice.** Snowden, D. J. and Boone, M. E. (2007). "A Leader's Framework for Decision Making." *Harvard Business Review* 85(11): 68–76, 149.

7. **Entrained thinking.** Ibid.

8. **Failed to anticipate.** Klein, G., Snowden, D., and Pin, C.L. "Anticipatory Thinking." *Proceedings of the Eighth International NDM Conference*, ed. K. Mosier & U. Fischer, Pacific Grove, CA, June 2007.

9. **Complicated decisions.** Snowden, D. J. and Boone, M. E. (2007). "A Leader's Framework for Decision Making." *Harvard Business Review* 85(11): 68–76, 149.

10. **VUCA inspired.** Bennis and Nanus discuss "how the leader designs and controls relationships with major constituencies in a complex, ambiguous, and uncertain environment." Bennis, W. and Nanus, B. (2007). *Leaders: The Strategies for Taking Charge* (Collins Business Essentials), 2nd ed. New York: Harper Business.

11. **What does VUCA mean?** Bennett, N. and Lemoine, J. (2014). "What VUCA really means for you." *Harvard Business Review* 92(1/2).

12. **The acronym VUCA.** Who first originated the term VUCA (Volatility, Uncertainty, Complexity and Ambiguity)? U.S. Army Heritage and Education Center. May 7, 2019. https://usawc.libanswers.com/faq/84869. Accessed September 20, 2020.

13. **Chess and VUCA.** McChrystal, G. S., et al. (2015). *Team of Teams: New Rules of Engagement for a Complex World.* New York: Portfolio/Penguin.

14. **Humble, open, and realistic leaders.** George, B. (2020). "These Coronavirus Heroes Show Us How Crisis Leadership Works." Harvard Business School, Working Knowledge Blog. March 24, 2020. https://hbswk.hbs.edu/item/these-coronavirus-heroes-show-us-how-crisis-leadership-works. Accessed September 9, 2020.

15. **Admit vulnerability.** Edmondson, A. C. and Chamorro-Premuzic, T. (2020). "Today's Leaders Need Vulnerability, Not Bravado." *Harvard Business Review.* October 9, 2020. https://hbr.org/2020/10/todays-leaders-need-vulnerability-not-bravado. Accessed November 9, 2020.

16. **Build resilience.** Sood, A. (2015). *The Mayo Clinic Handbook for Happiness: A Four-Step Plan for Resilient Living.* Boston, MA: Da Capo Press.

Chapter Three: Step Up to the Balcony

1. **Mindtraps.** Berger, J. G. (2019). *Unlocking Leadership Mindtraps: How to Thrive in Complexity.* Stanford, CA: Stanford University Press.

2. **Tami and Diane.** Asch, S. E. (1946). "Forming Impressions of Personality," *Journal of Abnormal and Social Psychology* 41: 258–90.

3. **Edict and persuasion.** Nutt, P. C. (1999). "Surprising but True: Half the Decisions in Organizations Fail." *Academy of Management Perspectives* 13(4): 75–90.

4. **Limiting assumptions.** Kegan R. and Lahey. L. L. "The Real Reason People Won't Change." *Harvard Business Review* November 2001. https://hbr.org/2001/11/the-real-reason-people-wont-change. Accessed July 4, 2021.

5. **Shackled ego.** Berger, J. G. (2019). *Unlocking Leadership Mindtraps: How to Thrive in Complexity.* Stanford, CA: Stanford University Press.

6. **Leadership without Easy Answers.** Heifetz, R. A. (1994). *Leadership without Easy Answers.* Cambridge, MA: Harvard University Press.

7. **Go to gain perspective, rather than to be seen.** McCullough, D. and McCullough, D. Jr. (2014). *You Are Not Special: And Other Encouragements.* New York: Ecco.

Chapter Four: Understand Burnout and Well-Being

1. **Language and metrics of burnout.** Maslach, C. and Jackson, S. E. (1981) "The Measurement of Experienced Burnout."

Journal of Organizational Behavior 2(2): 99–113.

2. **Definition of burnout.** Maslach, C. and Leiter, M. P. (2016). "Understanding the Burnout Experience: Recent Research and Its Implications for Psychiatry." *World Psychiatry* 15(2): 103–111.

3. **The extinguished candle of exhaustion.** Schaufeli, W.B., Leiter, M.P. and Maslach, C. (2009) "Burnout: 35 Years of Research and Practice." *Career Development International* 14(3): 204–220.

4. **Be positive, Glum.** *The Adventures of Gulliver* was a television cartoon produced by Hanna-Barbera Productions that first aired in 1968.

5. **Clinical burnout.** Roelofs, J., Verbraak, M., Keijsers, G. P., De Bruin, M. B., Schmidt, A. J. (2005) "Psychometric Properties of a Dutch Version of the Maslach Burnout Inventory General Survey (MBI-DV) in Individuals with and without Clinical Burnout." *Stress and Health: Journal of the International Society for the Investigation of Stress* 21(1): 17–25.

6. **Burnout versus simple exhaustion.** Ibid.

7. **Drivers of burnout.** Dyrbye, L. N., Shanafelt, T. D., Sinsky, C. A., et al. (2017) "Burnout Among Health Care Professionals: A Call to Explore and Address this Underrecognized Threat to Safe, High-Quality Care." *NAM Perspectives*. Discussion Paper, National Academy of Medicine, Washington, DC. https://nam.edu/burnout-among-health-care-professionals-a-call-to-explore-and-address-this-underrecognized-threat-to-safe-high-quality-care/

8. **Grit.** Duckworth, A. L., Peterson, C., Matthews, M. D., and Kelly, D. R. (2007)"Grit: Perseverance and Passion for Long-term Goals." *Journal of Personality and Social Psychology* 92(6): 1087.

9. **Exhaustion as a badge of honor.** Maslach, C. and Leiter, M. P. (2017). "Understanding Burnout: New Models." In *The Handbook of Stress and Health: A Guide to Research and Practice*, ed. Cary L. Cooper and James Campbell Quick (Newark, NJ: John Wiley & Sons.

10. **Repercussions of burnout.** Ibid.

11. **Six components of psychological well-being.** There are evolving discussions within academia regarding the relationships between psychological well-being, subjective well-being, eudaimonia, hedonia, and resilience. Ryff, C. D. and Keyes C. L. (1995) "The Structure of Psychological Well-being Revisited," *Journal of Personality and Social Psychology* 69(4): 719–27. Also, Ryff, C. D. (2014) "Psychological Well-being Revisited: Advances in the Science and Practice of Eudaimonia." *Psychotherapy and Psychosomatics* 83(1): 10–28.

12. **The mnemonic PAGERS.** Adapted from work by Carol Ryff. Physicians create mnemonics for almost everything. MUD-PILES is a mnemonic for the causes of metabolic acidosis. On, On, On, They Traveled And Found Voldemort Guarding Very Ancient Horcruxes is one of many mnemonics used to remember the names and the order of the twelve cranial nerves.

13. **Stress + Rest = Growth.** Stulberg, B. and Magness, S. (2017). *Peak Performance: Elevate Your Game, Avoid Burnout, and Thrive with the New Science of Success*. New York: Rodale.

14. **Creative thinker recovery and insight**. Csikszentmihalyi, M. (1996). *Creativity: Flow and the Psychology of Discovery and Invention*. New York: HarperCollins.

15. **World's worst boss.** Godin, S. "The World's Worst Boss." *Seth's Blog*. December 4, 2010. https://seths.blog/2010/12/the-worlds-worst-boss/. Accessed April 23, 2021.

16. **Well-being is a shared responsibility.** Shanafelt, T. D. and Noseworthy, J.H. (2017) "Executive Leadership and Physician Well-being: Nine Organizational Strategies to Promote Engagement and Reduce Burnout." *Mayo Clinic Proceedings* 92(1): 129–146.

17. **A shared responsibility including the board and leaders.** "Mayo Clinic Well-Being and Resiliency Resource Playbook."

18. **The Triple Aim.** Berwick, D. M., Nolan, T. W., and Whittington, J. "The Triple Aim: Care, Health, and Cost." *Health Affairs* (2008) 27(3): 759–769.

19. **The Quadruple Aim.** Bodenheimer, T. and Sinsky, C. "From Triple to Quadruple Aim: Care of the Patient Requires Care of the Provider." *The Annals of Family Medicine* (2014) 12(6): 573–576.

20. **The Maslach Burnout Inventory.** Maslach, C., Jackson, S. E., Leiter, M. P. *Maslach Burnout Inventory Manual*, 4th ed. Menlo Park, CA: Mind Garden: 2018.

21. **Two-item burnout assessment.** West, C. P., Dyrbye, L. N., Satele, D. V., Sloan, J. A., Shanafelt, T. D. "Concurrent Validity of Single-item Measures of Emotional Exhaustion and Depersonalization in Burnout Assessment." *Journal of General Internal Medicine* (2012) 27(11): 1445–52. DOI: 10.1007/s11606-012-2015-7.

Chapter Five: Amplify Engagement

1. **EHR rollouts gone wrong.** McCann, E. "EHR Rollouts Gone Wrong." *Healthcare IT News.* August 01, 2014. https://www.healthcareitnews.com/slideshow/ehr-rollouts-gone-wrong

2. **EHR rollouts gone wrong.** Schulte, F. and Fry, E. "Death By 1,000 Clicks: Where Electronic Health Records Went

Wrong." *Kaiser Health News.* March 18, 2019. https://khn. org/news/death-by-a-thousand-clicks/. Accessed December 26, 2020.

3. **Measure leadership behaviors.** Dr. Dyrbye's research team surveyed non-physician employees (nurses, business professionals, office staff, technicians, and other service and support personnel). Dyrbye, L. N., Major-Elechi, B., Hays, J. T., Fraser, C. H., Buskirk, S. J., and West, C. P. (2020) "Relationship Between Organizational Leadership and Health Care Employee Burnout and Satisfaction." *Mayo Clinic Proceedings* 95(4): 698–708.

4. **Leadership behaviors survey.** Mayo Clinic Participatory Management Leadership Score. Rochester, MN: Mayo Clinic.

5. **Leadership behavior effect on physicians.** Shanafelt, T. D., et al. (2015). "Impact of Organizational Leadership on Physician Burnout and Satisfaction." *Mayo Clinic Proceedings* 90(4): 432–440.

6. **Leader effect on work stress.** Harms, P., et al. (2017). "Leadership and Stress: A Meta-Analytic Review." *The Leadership Quarterly* 28(1): 178–194.

7. **Recognize what they do and who they are.** Robbins, M. "Why Employees Need Both Recognition and Appreciation." *Harvard Business Review*, November 12, 2019. https://hbr org/2019/11/why-employees-need-both-recognition-and-appreciation. Accessed March 13, 2021.

8. **Recognize outcomes that reflect excellence.** Buckingham, M. and Goodall, A. "The Feedback Fallacy." *Harvard Business Review.* (2019) 97(2): 92–101.

9. **No-stats all-stars.** Lewis, M. "The No-Stats All-Star." *New York Times Magazine.* February 13, 2009. https://

www.nytimes.com/2009/02/15/magazine/15Battier-t.html. Accessed March 13, 2021.

10. **You!** Rose, D. [@DanRose999]. (2021, March 12). "I frequently received emails from Sheryl with subject "You!" It might be a note (cc Mark) praising me for something. More often it was a note (cc me) to someone on my team (often deep in my org) praising them for something. Those little notes meant the world to their recipients." [Tweet]. Twitter. https://twitter.com/DanRose999/status/1370505963678035968. Accessed March 12, 2021.

11. **Leaders peer over the horizon.** Batista, E. "Leadership in Crisis (FDR and the Rubber Band Effect)" April 1, 2020. https://www.edbatista.com/2020/04/leadership-in-crisis-fdr-and-the-rubber-band-effect.html. Accessed January 8, 2021.

12. **The Rubber Band Effect.** Ibid.

13. **Practice values under pressure.** George, B. (2007). *True North: Discover Your Authentic Leadership.* San Francisco, California: Jossey-Bass.

14. **Culture = values + behavior.** I have seen this formula for culture often quoted. I am unsure of the original source. This is the earliest source I could find. Please reach out to me if you know of an earlier reference. Moore, C. A. (1980) "Major Definitions of the Concept of Culture: A Review of the Literature." https://eric.ed.gov/?id=ED229292. Page 25. Accessed March 24, 2021.

15. **Values are caught, not taught.** Whelan, E. and Dacy, M. D. (2017). *The Little Book of Mayo Clinic Values: A Field Guide for Your Journey.* Rochester, MN: Mayo Foundation for Medical Education and Research.

16. **Review of corporate values.** Sull, D., Turconi, S., and Sull, C. "When It Comes to Culture, Does Your Company Walk the Talk?" *MIT Sloan Management Review.* July 21, 2020. https://sloanreview.mit.edu/article/when-it-comes-to-culture-does-your-company-walk-the-talk/. Accessed July 26, 2020.

17. **Enron Code of Ethics.** Code of Ethics. Enron. July, 2000. https://www.justice.gov/archive/enron/exhibit/02-06/BBC-0001/Images/EXH012-02970.PDF. Accessed August 13, 2020.

18. **Enron fraud.** Barrionuevo, A. "Enron Chiefs Guilty of Fraud and Conspiracy." *New York Times.* May 25, 2006. https://www.nytimes.com/2006/05/25/business/25cnd-enron.html. Accessed August 13, 2020.

19. **Egosystem vs ecosystem.** Crocker, J. and Canevello, A. "From Egosystem to Ecosystem: Motivations of the Self in a Social World." In *Advances in Motivation Science*, ed. Andrew J. Elliot (Cambridge, MA: Elsevier 2018), 41–86.

20. **Egosystem vs ecosystem.** Kleon, A. "Further Notes on Scenius." May 12, 2017. https://austinkleon.com/2017/05/12/scenius/. Accessed December 28, 2020.

21. **Autonomy, competence, and supportive relationships.** Ryan, R. M. and Deci, E. L. "On Happiness and Human Potentials: A Review of Research on Hedonic and Eudaimonic Well-Being." *Annual Review of Psychology* (2001) 52(1): 141–66.

22. **The University of Minnesota Physicians and Keyhubs.** "Leverage Hidden Influencers." https://www.keyhubs.com/case-studies/leverage-hidden-influencers-to-improve-culture-case-study-2/. Accessed March 30, 2021.

23. **Communal creativity.** Ogilvy, J. A. (2002). *Creating Better*

Futures: Scenario Planning As a Tool for a Better Tomorrow.
New York: Oxford University Press.

24. **Leaders at all levels.** Swensen, S., et al. (2016). "Leadership by Design: Intentional Organization Development of Physician Leaders." *Journal of Management Development* 35(4): 549–570.

25. **Genius is individual.** Jeffries, S. "Surrender. It's Brian Eno." *Guardian.* April 28, 2010. https://www.theguardian.com/music/2010/apr/28/brian-eno-brighton-festival. Accessed December 28, 2020.

26. **Scenius is communal.** Eno, B. (1996). *A Year with Swollen Appendices: Brian Eno's Diary.* London, England: Faber & Faber Ltd.

27. **Conjuring scenius.** McCormick, P. "Conjuring scenius." *The Packy McCormick Blog,* May 17, 2020. https://www.packym.com/blog/conjuring-scenius. Accessed March 29, 2021.

28. **Inklings.** Plaskitt, E. "Inklings." *Oxford Dictionary of National Biography.* September 28, 2006. https://doi.org/10.1093/ref:odnb/92544. Accessed March 29, 2021.

29. **We were no mutual admiration society.** Schakel, P. "Inklings." *Encyclopedia Britannica,* 29 May 2016. https://www.britannica.com/topic/Inklings. Accessed March 29, 2021.

30. **Best-selling fantasy books.** Parker, G. "The 20 Best-Selling Fantasy Books of All-Time." *Money Inc.* 2019. https://moneyinc.com/best-selling-fantasy-books-of-all-time/. Accessed March 29, 2021.

31. **Building 20.** Hilts, P. "Last Rites for a 'Plywood Palace' That Was a Rock of Science." *New York Times.* March 31, 1998. https://www.nytimes.com/1998/03/31/science/last-rites-

for-a-plywood-palace-that-was-a-rock-of-science.html. Accessed March 29, 2021.

32. **Key elements of scenius.** Kelly, K. "Scenius, or Communal Genius." June 10, 2018. https://kk.org/thetechnium/scenius-or-comm/. Accessed December 12, 2020.

33. **Individuals within a scenius look at each other's work.** Kleon, A. (2014). *Show Your Work!* New York: Workman Publishing.

34. **Leadership behavior survey.** Mayo Clinic Participatory Management Leadership Score. Rochester, MN: Mayo Clinic.

35. **Recognize what they do and who they are.** Robbins, M. "Why Employees Need Both Recognition and Appreciation." *Harvard Business Review.* November 12, 2019. https://hbr org/2019/11/why-employees-need-both-recognition-and-appreciation. Accessed March 13, 2021.

36. **Culture is the sum of its values plus behavior.** Moore, C. A. (1980) "Major Definitions of the Concept of Culture: A Review of the Literature." https://eric.ed.gov/?id=ED229292. Page 25. Accessed March 24, 2021.

37. **Values are caught, not taught.** Whelan, E. and Dacy, M. D. (2017). *The Little Book of Mayo Clinic Values: A Field Guide for Your Journey.* Rochester, Minnesota: Mayo Foundation for Medical Education and Research.

Chapter Six: Lead During One-to-One Conversations

1. **The Five Hats of Effective Leaders.** This concept builds upon the work of my MBA and executive coaching professors, Robert Hicks and John McCracken, from the University of Texas at Dallas, who published a paper about the three hats

of a leader. (Hicks, R. and McCracken, J. (2010) "Three Hats of a Leader: Coaching, Mentoring and Teaching." *Physician Executive Journal* 36(6): 68–70). I further extended the concept through the help of discussions with my friends and close colleagues Drs. Brad Barth, from the University of Kansas, and Teresa Chan, from McMaster University.

2. **Leadership is lifting a person's vision.** Drucker, P. F. (2008). *Management, Revised Edition.* New York: Collins.

3. **Mentoring vs teaching.** Hicks, R. and McCracken, J. (2010) "Three Hats of a Leader: Coaching, Mentoring and Teaching." *Physician Executive Journal* 36(6): 68–70.

4. **Personal growth and reconciling different perspectives.** Kegan, R. (1995). *In Over Our Heads: The Mental Demands of Modern Life.* Cambridge, MA: Harvard University Press.

5. **The GROW Model of coaching.** Whitmore, J. (2017). *Coaching for Performance: Growing Human Potential and Purpose: The Principles and Practice of Coaching and Leadership.* Boston, MA: Nicholas Brealey Publishing.

6. **Jules and Watts.** A power metaphor. Also, the Hiwatt CP103 was an amplifier favored by Pete Townshend during the early years of the band The Who.

7. **Generalizations, deletions, distortions.** Bandler, R. and Grinder, J. (1975). *The Structure of Magic.* Vol. 1. Palo Alto, CA: Science and Behavior Books.

8. **Vincent and Jules.** *Pulp Fiction* anyone?

Chapter Eight: Document Your Perspectives

1. **Harrison Bergeron.** Vonnegut, K. (2014). *Welcome to the Monkey House: The Special Edition.* New York: Dial Press.

2. **Deep thinking.** Newport, C. (2019). *Digital Minimalism:*

Choosing a Focused Life in a Noisy World. New York: Port-folio/Penguin.

Chapter Nine: Create a Shared Reality

1. **What is water?** Wallace, D. F. (2009). *This Is Water: Some Thoughts, Delivered on a Significant Occasion, about Living a Compassionate Life*. New York: Little, Brown and Company.
2. **Develop wisdom.** Kegan, R. (1982). *The Evolving Self*. Cambridge, MA: Harvard University Press.
3. **Challenge own perspectives.** Eigel, K. (1998). "Leader Effectiveness: A Constructive Developmental View and Investigation." PhD Dissertation. Advisor: Kuhnert, K. Athens: University of Georgia.
4. **The Wisdom of Crowds.** Surowiecki, J. (2005). *The Wisdom of Crowds*. New York: Anchor Books.
5. **Leadership triads.** Swensen, S., Gorringe, G., Caviness, J. and Peters, D. (2016) "Leadership by Design: Intentional Organization Development of Physician Leaders." *Journal of Management Development* 35(4): 549–570.
6. **Dyads and triads.** At times there are leadership dyads or triads. Whether there is a leadership dyad or a triad depends on the work unit; patient-care-oriented work units, such as cardiology, tend to operate with leadership triads that include a nurse leader, whereas other work units, such as research or education, tend to operate with leadership dyads that include a physician or scientist and an administrator.
7. **Team diversity.** Díaz-García, C., González-Moreno, A. and Jose Saez-Martinez, F., 2013. "Gender Diversity within R&D Teams: Its Impact on Radicalness of Innovation." *Innovation* 15(2): 149–160.

8. **Team diversity.** Herring, C. (2009). "Does Diversity Pay? Race, Gender, and the Business Case for Diversity." *American Sociological Review* 74(2): 208–224.

9. **Team diversity.** Levine, S. S., Apfelbaum, E. P., Bernard, M., Bartelt, V. L., Zajac, E. J. and Stark, D. (2014) "Ethnic Diversity Deflates Price Bubbles." *Proceedings of the National Academy of Sciences* 111(52): 18524–18529.

10. **Team diversity.** Hunt, V., Layton, D. and Prince, S. (2015) "Diversity Matters." *McKinsey & Company* 1(1): 15–29.

11. **Team diversity.** Rock, D. and Grant, H. (2016) "Why Diverse Teams Are Smarter." *Harvard Business Review* 4(4): 2–5.

Chapter Ten: Identify Fears and Worries

1. **Beowulf.** Heaney, S., trans. (2009). *Beowulf: A New Verse Translation.* New York: W.W. Norton & Company.

2. **The monsters surface at night.** Whyte, D. (1996). *The Heart Aroused: Poetry and the Preservation of the Soul in Corporate America.* New York: Currency Doubleday.

3. **Jerry Colonna.** Colonna, J. (2019). *Reboot: Leadership and the Art of Growing Up.* New York: HarperBusiness.

4. **The monster in your head.** Colonna, J. "Monster." *The Monster in Your Head Blog.* http://web.archive.org/web/20100202034946/http://www.themonsterinyourhead.com/2010/01/28/monsters. Accessed May 13, 2021.

5. **Immunity to Change.** Kegan, R. and Lahey, L. L. (2009) *Immunity to Change: How to Overcome It and Unlock Potential in Yourself and Your Organization.* Boston, MA: Harvard Business Press.

6. **Interrupting leader.** Wanting to interrupt less or—the opposite—wanting to speak up more are common goals for many leaders.

7. **Identify fears and worries.** Kegan R. and Lahey, L. L. "The real reason people won't change." *Harvard Business Review* November 2001, https://hbr.org/2001/11/the-real-reason-people-wont-change. Accessed July 4, 2021.

8. **My coaching research.** Notes I have taken while coaching leaders both inside and outside of Mayo Clinic.

Chapter Eleven: Create a Shared Vision

1. **Top 10 core values of corporations.** Sull, D., Turconi, S., and Sull, C. "When It Comes to Culture, Does Your Company Walk the Talk?" *MIT Sloan Management Review.* July 21, 2020. https://sloanreview.mit.edu/article/when-it-comes-to-culture-does-your-company-walk-the-talk/. Accessed July 26, 2020.

2. **The mission of Quaker Oats.** "Since 1877, [Quaker Oats has] been on a mission to inspire health, fitness and energy amongst our patrons." https://quaker.co.in/about-us. Accessed August 19, 2020.

Chapter Twelve: Generate Multiple Options

1. **The Ohio State University.** My wife graduated from The Ohio State University. I mentioned The Ohio State University twice previously in the book. This endnote brings the count up to four. Also, note the capital "The" before Ohio State University. Apparently, that is their thing. I attended college at the University of Illinois at Chicago with the "the" in the lowercase.

2. **Half the decisions of organizations fail.** Nutt, P. C. (1999). "Surprising but True: Half the Decisions in Organizations Fail." *Academy of Management Perspectives* 13(4): 75–90.

3. **Success rate of decisions.** Success was defined as sustained

adoption of the decision. Ninety-seven of the decisions considered a single option and forty of them considered multiple options. (p ≤ 0.01) Nutt, P. C. (1993). "The Identification of Solution Ideas during Organizational Decision Making." *Management Science* 39(9): 1071–1085.

4. **The Vanishing Options Test and the Eccentric Genie.** Heath, C. and D. Heath. (2013). *Decisive: How to Make Better Choices in Life and Work.* New York: Currency.

5. **Glum.** Here is a YouTube video of Glum from *The Adventures of Gulliver* in action: https://youtu.be/2KvNt5NG-GM. Accessed July 11, 2021.

6. **First followers.** Sivers, D. "First Follower: Leadership Lessons from a Dancing Guy." https://sive.rs/ff. Accessed July 11, 2021.

7. **The tie vote.** I first heard this joke from Dr. Greg Henry. Dr. Henry is a Clinical Professor of Emergency Medicine at the University of Michigan and a past president of the American College of Emergency Physicians.

Chapter Thirteen: Champion the Way Forward

1. **OKR origin.** Pines, G. "The OKR Origin Story." https://www.whatmatters.com/articles/the-origin-story/ June 4, 2018. Accessed May 16, 2021.

2. **Directly Responsible Individual (DRI).** Lashinsky, A. (2012). *Inside Apple: How America's Most Admired—and Secretive—Company Really Works.* New York: Business Plus.

3. **Matrix organizations.** Davis, S. M. and Lawrence, P.R. (1978). "Problems of Matrix Organizations." *Harvard Business Review* 56(3): 131–142.

4. **Self-managing organizations.** Bernstein, E., et al. (2016).

"Beyond the Holacracy Hype." *Harvard Business Review* 94(7/8): 38–49.

5. **Do-Be-Do-Be-Do.** Thanks to Diane Margaret Twedell, DNP, MS, RN, CENP, for her quick wit.

6. **Even optimal decisions can fail.** Success was defined as sustained adoption of the decision. Ninety-seven of the decisions considered a single option, and forty of them considered multiple options. (p ≤ 0.01) Nutt, P. C. (1993). "The Identification of Solution Ideas during Organizational Decision Making." *Management Science* 39(9): 1071–1085.

7. **Streamlining Hotel Housekeeping.** Weed, J. "Streamlining Hotel Housekeeping in a Tight Labor Market." *New York Times*, November 26, 2019. https://www.nytimes.com/2019/11/26/business/hotel-housekeepers.html. Accessed September 19, 2020.

Chapter Fourteen: Now What?

1. **Ideas are multipliers of execution.** Derek Sivers. "Ideas Are Just Multipliers of Execution. https://sive.rs/multiply. August 16, 2005. Accessed January 30, 2022.

2. **A union of forces.** Mayo, William J. (1910) Rush Medical School Graduation Speech. Rochester. MN: Mayo Clinic Historical Unit.

INDEX

Page references in italics indicate figures, and t *indicates a table.*

accountability as a corporate value, 237
The Adventures of Gulliver, 77–78, 294n4
Ali, Muhammad, 180
Asch, Solomon, 65
autonomy, 82, 86, 98

Batista, Ed, 108–9
Bennis, W., 292n10
Beowulf, 219
blind spots, 62–63, 67, 71, 73
Blue Earth Healthy Living Clinic, 33, 54–55
Buckingham, Marcus, 104–5
Building 20 (Massachusetts Institute of Technology), 119
burnout
  causes of, 78–79, 88
  confidential data on, 89
  as cynicism, 77
  definition of, 77–78
  and efficacy levels, 84

as emotional exhaustion, 77–78
importance of, 80
leadership behaviors' impact on, 97–98, 101
measuring/evaluating survey results, 88–91
and meditation, 85–86
myths about, 92
organizational level of efficacy, 88–92
overview and summary of, 11, 76–77, 93–94
rate of, 76, 88
and running/exercise, 85
See also well-being, psychological

chaos, 56–57
  acting with urgency, 50
  admitting vulnerability, 51
  backchannel communication, 52
  celebrating people/accomplishments, 52
  decisions in chaotic environments, 48–50

delegating decisions, 51
deliberate focus, 51
  and human impact of
    decisions, recognizing,
    52–53
  leveraging your leadership
    team, 50–51
  and mission/values,
    amplifying, 52
  transparent communication,
    51–52
coaching, 103, 135–46, 154t
Cognitive Edge, 35
collaboration as a corporate
  value, 237
Colonna, Jerry, 220
communication as a corporate
  value, 113
complex challenges, 8–9, 179–83
confrontation, 68
customer as a corporate value,
  237

decision-making
  benchmark decisions, 116
  diversity in, 197–98
  by edict, 7–8, 69, 289n1
  mapping (*see* mapping
    decisions)
  reflexive (*see* expertise)
Decisive (the Heaths), 248, 289n3
disagreement, 41, 68–69, 199, 254

diversity, 197–99, 237
Doerr, John, 258
Drucker, Peter, 128
Dyrbye, Lotte, 97–98, 297n3

EHR (electronic health record),
  27, 95–96, 116, 123–24
engagement, 95–126
  core values, embodying,
    111–14
  developing colleagues, 101–4
  egosystems vs. ecosystems,
    115–18
  engaging colleagues, 114–20
  and helicopter leaders, 101
  informing colleagues, 108–11
  leadership behaviors, 97–100,
    122–23, 297n3
  one-to-one conversations,
    102
  overview and summary of,
    11–12, 95–96, 124–26
  plus-minus measurement of
    colleagues, 105–6
  recognizing colleagues,
    104–8
  respecting colleagues,
    120–21
  scenius (group wisdom),
    118–19
  supervising colleagues,
    121–22

supervising yourself, 122–23

tracking interactions with
colleagues, 102–3

via coaching, 103

via group learning, 103

Eno, Brian, 118

Enron, 113

environmental mastery,
82, 86

excellence as a corporate value,
113, 237

expertise, 18–32

analysis pitfalls, 28–29

disagreement among experts,
41

overplaying, 22–25, 29

overview and summary of,
10–11, 18–19, 31–32

people as decision-making
robots, 19–22

process vs. analysis, 26–28

putting the breaks on,
30–31

in Snapple decision (case
study), 25–26

sought out for complicated
decisions, 40–41

vs. the VUCA environment,
46–47, 47t

Face/Off, 191

Farrugia, Gianrico, 49

fears and worries, 218–31

Beowulf example, 219

blaming yourself when bad
things happen, 225

brought into a shared reality,
230

common, list of, 223–24

feedback to colleagues,
226

Immunity to Change
investigation,
221–27

leaving struggling colleagues
to fend for themselves,
227

losing respect of colleagues,
226

losing your job due to low
productivity, 226

making others' priorities your
own, 226

micromanaging, 225

mitigating, 238–39

the monsters in our head,
220, 222

of organizations, 227–29

overview and summary of,
13, 166, 218, 231

pushing yourself in order to
grow, 226

Freaky Friday, 191

Garvey Berger, Jennifer
    *Unlocking Leadership
    Mindtraps*, 63
Gatorade, 25
George, Bill, 111
Godin, Seth, 88
Goodall, Ashley, 104–5
Grove, Andy, 258
GROW model of coaching,
    136–40

Hanna-Barbera Productions,
    294n4
"Harrison Bergeron" (Vonnegut),
    177
Heath, Chip and Dan
    Decisive, 248, 289n3
Heifetz, Ronald
    *Leadership Without Easy
    Answers*, 71
Henry, Greg, 306n7
Hicks, Robert, 289n1, 301–2n1

ideas converted to action,
    280–81
Inklings, 118–19
innovation as a corporate value,
    237
integrity as a corporate value,
    113, 237

Magness, Steve
    Peak Performance, 87

job satisfaction. *See* burnout;
    well-being, psychological

Kegan, Robert, 221
    "The Real Reason People
    Won't Change," 71
Kelly, Kevin, 119
Keyhubs, 116–17
Kleon, Austin, 115

Lahey, Lisa Laskow, 221
    "The Real Reason People
    Won't Change," 71
Lashinsky, Adam, 262
leadership
    behaviors of, 97–99
    deciding how you will lead,
        280–81
    Five Hats approach, overview
        of, 128–30, 301–2n1 (*see
        also under* one-to-one
        conversations)
    GRR! model of, 147–49
    reasons for, 15
    titles/formal roles, 115
Leadership Without Easy Answers
    (Heifetz), 71
Lewis, C.S, 119
Lewis, Warren, 118–19

mapping decisions, 33–60
 in ambiguous situations,
  45–46
 best practices, 37–39
 clear domains, 35, 35–39,
  37, 56
 complex decisions, 35, 36,
  45, 47–48, 47t, 53–54,
  56
 complicated domains, 35, 36,
  40–42, 56
 confused decisions, 35,
  54–56
 Cynefin decision domains,
  34–42, 35, 289–90n3
 and entrained thinking, 39,
  41, 46
 and overanalysis, 41–42
 overview and summary of,
  11, 33–34, 58–60
 in uncertain situations,
  44–45
 volatile environments, 44
 VUCA decision domains,
  43–48, 47t, 53–58,
  292n10 (see also chaos)
Maslach Burnout Inventory
 (MBI), 90
matrix organizations, 263–64
Mayo, William J., 281
MBI (Maslach Burnout
 Inventory), 90

McCracken, John, 301–2n1
McKinsey Quarterly, 26
mentoring, 133–35, 154t
"Minnesota nice," 68
mnemonics, 83, 295n12

Nanus, B., 292n10
Nutt, Paul, 69, 166, 244, 272

Ogilvy, James, 118
Olson, Shelly, 30
one-to-one conversations,
 127–57
 coaching, 135–46, 154t
 engagement via, 102
 Five Hats approach,
  overview of, 128–30,
  301–2n1
 mentoring, 133–35, 154t
 overview and summary of,
  12, 127–28, 155–57
 phrases to explore, 141–45
 sponsoring, 150–51, 154t
 supervising, 146–50,
  154t
 teaching, 130–33, 153t
 wearing multiple hats in,
  151–53, 153–54t
options, generating, 243–56
 categories of options,
  247–48
 doing nothing, 246–47

leader as decision-maker, 254–55

multiple options, 166, 244–47, 305–6n3

overview and summary of, 14, 243–44, 255–56

and pessimism, 251–52

and resistance, 253

selecting options to pursue, 166, 251

and the silent majority, 252–53

tie votes, 254

time needed for, 171

vanishing options, 248–50

Peak Performance (Stulberg and Magness), 87

people as a corporate value, 237

personal growth, 82, 86–87

personality traits, 198

perspective, 61–75

agreement, 68–69

biases/mindtraps, overview of, 62–63

blind spots, 62–63, 67, 71, 73

control, 69–70

dance floor/metaphor for broadening, 71–73, 175–76

ego and self-limiting assumptions, 70–71

overview and summary of, 11, 61–62, 74–75

problems with your perspective, 62

rightness, 66–67

simple stories, 63–66

perspectives, documenting, 175–93

body swapping with others/empathizing, 191

and creating a shared reality, 175–76 (*see also* shared reality, creating)

expanding your perspective, 186–89 (*see also* perspective)

identifying a complex challenge, 179–83

identifying themes in your thoughts, 189–91

overview and summary of, 12–13, 165, 175–76, 192–93

time and space to think, 176–79

writing down your thoughts, 183–86

purpose, 82, 86, 98

Quadruple Aim, 89

Quaker Oats, 25–26, 239–40,
    245–46

reality. *See* shared reality,
    creating
"The Real Reason People Won't
    Change" (Kegan and Lahey),
    71
reflexive decision making. *See*
    expertise
relationships, positive, 82, 86, 98
respect, 113, 120–21, 237
rest/recovery and growth, 87
Rose, Dan, 106–7
ROW Forward framework,
    160–74
    and cognitive headlock, 163
    finance committee example,
        160–63, 172–73
    overview and summary of,
        12, 160, 164, *165,* 174
    time and scope for, 168–71
    a typical confused meeting,
        172–73
    See also options, generating;
        perspectives,
        documenting; shared
        reality, creating; the way
        forward
Rubber Band Effect, 108–9
Ryff, Carol, 82–83, 90

Sandberg, Sheryl, 106–7
self-acceptance, 82, 86
self-managed organizations,
    264
shared reality, creating, 194–217
    and broadening your
        perspectives, 214–15
        (*see also* perspective)
    and creating a shared vision,
        238–40
    and diverse opinions,
        197–99
    and documenting
        perspectives, 175–76
    documenting perspectives
        electronically, 202–7
    documenting perspectives
        of groups in person,
        208–14
    documenting perspectives
        through interviews,
        207–8
    and independent opinions,
        200–201
    overview and summary of,
        13, 165–66, 194–95,
        201–2, 215–17
    time needed for, 171
    and the wisdom of effective
        leaders, 195–96
    and the wisdom of the team,
        196–97

See also fears and worries;
    perspectives,
    documenting; shared
    vision, creating
shared vision, creating, 232–42
    and creating a shared reality,
        238–40
    creating a vision statement,
        234–35
    fears/worries, mitigating,
        238–39
    mission/values, amplifying,
        236–38
    overview and summary of,
        13–14, 166, 232–33,
        241–42
    Quaker Oats (case study),
        239–40
Shrek the Third, 191
Sivers, Derek, 280
Snapple, 25–26, 239, 245–46
Snowden, David, 35, 290n3
social responsibility as a
    corporate value, 237
Stern, Howard, 25–26
stress, 87, 98
Stulberg, Brad
    Peak Performance, 87
success, factors affecting,
    114
Sull, Charles, 236–37
Sull, Donald, 236–37

supervising, 121–23, 146–50,
    154t
Surowiecki, James, 196

teaching, 130–33, 153t
teamwork, 112
Tolkien, J.R.R., 119
Trastek, Victor, 21–22, 25, 30–31
Triple Aim, 89
Turconi, Stefano, 236–37

Unlocking Leadership Mindtraps
    (Garvey Berger), 63

values/culture, organizational,
    111–14, 236–38
vision. See shared vision, creating
Vonnegut, Kurt
    "Harrison Bergeron," 177

the way forward, 257–79
    addressing scheduling, 167,
        266–68
    boutique hotel (case study),
        276–78
    delegating tasks, 167,
        268–71
    the directly responsible
        individual (DRI),
        appointing, 167, 261–65
    iterations of moving
        forward, 274–75

learning fast/failing fast, 272, 307n6

metrics, 259

milestones, 260–61

objectives and key results (OKRs), identifying, 167, 258–61

the objective team (OT), choosing, 167, 265–66

overview and summary of, 14, 167–68, 257–58, 278–79

sharing your findings, 273–74

time needed for planning, 171

tracking boards, 272–73

See also ROW Forward framework

well-being, psychological, 80–91

confidential data on, 89

and diet, 86

dimensions of, 82–83, 90

and efficacy levels, overview of, 84

growth equation, 87

individual level of efficacy, 85–88

interpersonal level of efficacy, 92–93

leadership behaviors' impact on, 98

measuring/evaluating survey results, 88–91

and meditation, 85–86

mnemonic PAGERs for, 83

organizational level of efficacy, 88–92

overview and summary of, 80–82, 93–94

and running/exercise, 85–87

and sleep, 86

vs. subjective well-being, eudaimonia, hedonia, and resilience, 295n11

See also burnout

Whitmore, Sir John, 136

Yuen Mei Ching Yan, 191

CREDITS AND PERMISSIONS